HEEL AND TOE

THE CLIMBS OF GREATER VEDAUWOO, WYOMING

*Being in such a place is unlike any other place you could be:
the fact that a human being could be in such a place climbing,
moving upward, being in control, still making rational decisions
is a very exciting and almost mystical experience.*
Roger Briggs

HEEL AND TOE

THE CLIMBS OF GREATER VEDAUWOO, WYOMING

Skip Harper • Rob Kelman

HEEL and TOE Publishers
Fort Collins, Colorado

Published by
Heel and Toe Publishers
1312 Robertson St.
Fort Collins, CO 80524-4258

All photographs and illustrations by Skip Harper unless indicated otherwise.
Logo by Mary Babcock.

Manufactured in the United States of America

Front Cover Photograph: Steve Bechtel on *SpectreMan*.
Frontispiece: Jim Brink working on a project in an outlying area.

Publisher's Cataloging in Publication
  (Prepared by Quality Books Inc.)

Harper, Skip.
    Heel and toe: the climbs of Greater Vedauwoo, Wyoming/Skip Harper, Rob Kelman.
    p. cm.
    Includes bibliographical references and index.
    Preassigned LCCN: 94-075804
    ISBN 0-9640645-0-2
    1. Rock climbing--Wyoming--Medicine Bow National Forest-- Guidebooks. 2. Medicine Bow National Forest (Wyo.) -- Guidebooks.
    I. Kelman, Rob. II. Title

GV199.42.W86M434 1994   917.8786
                               QBI 94-648

In Memoriam

We dedicate this book to the memory of Layne Kopischka -- who for over seventeen years created a series of guidebooks to Vedauwoo. Our book builds on the foundation that he laid. On a more personal note, he taught us how to climb here, in particular how to manage offwidths, and encouraged our efforts over the years as we struggled on Vedauwoo routes and complained to him about his ratings. His reasoned opinions and strongly held convictions remain an integral part of our Vedauwoo experience. We have felt his presence looking over our shoulders as we have written this book. As we have changed a rating or modified a route description, we have often thought about what he would have said. Given the difference in our approach from that which he championed, we can well imagine his saying, "You guys are all wet about that. But, what the heck, go for it. You don't know any better."

ALERT!
Read this before using this book.
Climbing is a dangerous sport.
Climbers are injured and die pursuing this activity.

Our purpose in writing this guide is to document the existence of various climbs, and to present enough descriptive information so as to enable the climbs to be located. The guide is a compilation of information the authors have gathered from their own experience, from many other climbers and from many other sources. We (the authors) did not prepare summaries of our climbs immediately afterwards, and we did not attempt to verify all information obtained from other sources. Our opinions concerning the technical difficulties and ratings of the climbs are subjectively our own and may differ from the opinions of others. The information may or may not be entirely accurate. Therefore, no one reading this guide should rely upon the information it contains in deciding whether and how to climb any route described herein. Whether or not you decide to use this information to climb is solely and entirely at your own discretion.

Under no circumstance should any reader depend on the information contained in this book for personal safety or for determining whether to attempt any climb or route described.

The condition of the climber, and the condition of the climb are unique each day. The difficulty to be experienced by each climber depends upon that climber's height, weight, reach, strength, level of physical fitness and diet, as well as that climber's knowledge, experience and ability. There are always risks involved in climbing from all manner of changing circumstances including, but not limited to, the condition of the rock, breaking holds, falling objects such as rock and gear, inadequate or faulty gear, climate, weather and failure of fixed protection. Accordingly, any reader who undertakes to climb any of the routes described on these pages should not rely on the material presented herein, but on his or her own judgment about the climb and the resulting steps to be taken to minimize the risks involved.

You are responsible for your actions. You must evaluate every climb relative to your ability and all other circumstances. Should you have any doubt about any climb, do not attempt to climb it.

At best, this guide provides information for you to use in determining whether or not to investigate any climb or route further, and should only be used in conjunction with your judgment and on-site observations. The authors suggest consulting with other climbers for advice, particularly those living nearby. Also, you should consult or engage a qualified/certified instructor for assistance in developing safe technique and knowledge of the climbs and routes and the particular hazards that may be encountered. For example, some of the routes in this book may have bolts, pitons or other hardware already in place in the rock. Because of weathering, metal fatigue and other factors, use of such 'fixed protection' should be backed up by other equipment. The existence, reliability and use of any fixed protection should be investigated in advance.

In short, any reader using the information in this book to plan or execute a climb on any particular route does so at his or her own risk.

THE AUTHORS MAKE NO WARRANTIES, EXPRESS OR IMPLIED, OF ANY KIND; IN PARTICULAR, THE AUTHORS DO NOT WARRANT THAT THE INFORMATION IN THIS BOOK IS WHOLLY ACCURATE OR RELIABLE. FURTHER, THE AUTHORS MAKE NO WARRANTIES OF FITNESS FOR PARTICULAR PURPOSE OR THAT THE INFORMATION CONTAINED IS IN ANYWAY MERCHANTABLE.

Table of Contents

Johnna Tipton happily "heel and toeing" on the notorious sandbag, *Upper Slot* **(5.7+)**

Introduction

"...the hearsay nature of much climbing information makes a totally accurate guidebook impossible." Jim Erickson in *Rocky Heights*, 1980.

"Indians must have climbed many of the natural lines in the park. With the natural climbability of the rock, many young braves may have ventured into the vertical unknown as a test of their manhood [and probably many young maidens just for the fun of it -- SH and RK]. It is with this historical perspective that we, the authors, have left all of the routes in this book unattributed." James Crump, David Head, and Mike Head in *Indian Heights,* 1985.

For the small percentage of you who actually read introductions, we will keep it short and to the point. *Heel and Toe* is a guidebook to Greater Vedauwoo. This includes the Central Area around Vedauwoo Glen and many of the outlying areas such as Blair. We plan to expand coverage in future editions.

The primary purpose of a guidebook is to direct the reader to the climb, provide a moderately accurate description of the route, an estimate of its rating, and any significant special considerations such as peculiarities of protection or seasonal closures to protect wildlife. It is precisely these elements that are emphasized in this guide. All other considerations such as history, geology, and local color are secondary and optional. Sometimes they are fun and interesting while at other times distracting and annoying. Readers interested in a fulsome analysis of the purposes and philosophy of writing guidebooks should consult the definitive articles by Randy Vogel cited in the Bibliography.

We do not provide a précis of the geology of Vedauwoo. Most climbers are content to know that the cliffs are composed of rock and whether it is smooth or rough, solid or rotten. We do provide that information. Items 2 and 8 in the Bibliography are good sources to find out more about the geology of southeastern Wyoming. Item 25 is an extensive, scholarly description of the geology of Wyoming.

When wired stoppers were first introduced, many British purists objected on several grounds. One of them was that it would no longer be possible to distinguish between a free ascent and an aid ascent. They reasoned that once you could easily place protection above yourself, you would, at critical junctions, be climbing with a top rope. We do not subscribe to that degree of ethical purity. However, the point is well taken that once the game became getting to the top by a special set of rules rather than just getting to the top, controversy surrounded first ascents.

This is not a new phenomenon but has dogged the assignment of credit and discredit in free climbing for decades. Vedauwoo is no stranger to this situation. Not wishing to make judgments is one reason we have hesitated to include the names of first ascensionists. Also, no first ascent credit has been given in any Vedauwoo guidebook for over two decades, and, in fact, no verbal descriptions of the routes have been given. This gap in formally maintained records creates a considerable obstacle in designating first ascensionists and sometimes even the name of the climb. Further, we ascribe to Napoleon's dictum, "History is fiction agreed upon." (Actually there is debate over whether he did say that!)

For all these reasons and because of our own tepid interest in the subject, we do not furnish first ascent information in this edition. See the article by Ed Webster in the Bibliography for a strong defense of including historical material in a guidebook. We should mention that many references in the Bibliography do contain historical material about climbing at Vedauwoo.

ACKNOWLEDGMENTS

J.C. Halfpenny's 1971 book, *A Climber's Guide To Southeastern Wyoming,* had a visionary concept of climbing in the Greater Vedauwoo Area. This remarkable book has been a source of data and inspiration for us with its carefully crafted verbal and pictorial descriptions of early climbing at Vedauwoo.

We appreciate all the help that our friends in Wyoming have given to us, a couple of greenies from Colorado. In particular, Steve Bechtel, Scott Blunk, and Tim Rangitsch have answered many requests for information. An especial thanks goes to Bob Scarpelli whose exploits and knowledge of Vedauwoo are without parallel. His 1987 guidebook, *The Cracksmen,* which covers the outlying areas of Vedauwoo, has been a valuable resource in crafting this book. In addition, early on he accompanied us in walking tours of the outlying areas which greatly advanced the writing of the book. Paul Piana has been unflinchingly generous in his support of this project. He supplied us with numerous slides, written descriptions, and conversations illuminating climbing activities at Vedauwoo during the past 20 years.

RK extends his appreciation to Jim Brink, Andy Kovats, Willi Miller, and Robert Warren with whom he has enjoyed many happy days of climbing at Vedauwoo. Much of what he learned about Vedauwoo came from these experiences.

GRAPHICS

Most of the graphics used for this book originated as standard 35 mm B/W photographs or color transparencies. Approximately 60 were halftoned before final printing. Another 60 or so were digitized either by Skip Harper using Logitech hardware or by Cimarron International Graphics, Inc., Denver. Using Aldus Photostyler Software, each electronic file was imported into an Intel 486 based PC with 16 megabytes of RAM and 256K cache. Images were retouched for desired results. Some images were further reworked with one or more of the following: Aldus Effects filters, Photomorph (North Coast Software), Imagine (Impulse, Inc.) software. Images were archived on either Colorado Memory Systems tape or SyQuest Cartridge. All final graphics were stored on SyQuest Cartridge and were output through an image setter to linotronic negatives at 4000 dpi. Final printing was at 150 linescreen.

COMMENTS, CORRECTIONS, ADDITIONS

If you have any comments, corrections or additions to make, they can be sent to

Rob Kelman
Heel and Toe Publishers
1312 Robertson St.
Fort Collins CO 80524-4258
FAX: (303)493-4496 || Voice: (303)482-0974

Information can also be placed in the new route book at Tim's Outdoor Store, 412 Grand Ave., Laramie WY. We welcome information about the name of first ascensionists which may (or may not) make its way into a future edition. We have not always had an easy time in chasing down the correct name for a route. Please let us know, if you feel a different name should have been used. We even welcome your comments on our route descriptions and ratings.

1. Where, What, Why and Warnings

This chapter provides general background information about Vedauwoo, safety and emergency services, explanations of route descriptions, and a bibliography. We urge you to read this chapter before starting to use the book, especially if you are new to the area. If you choose not to read this chapter prior to climbing at Vedauwoo, you assume all risks associated with such inaction. The name is pronounced Vee'-da-voo and comes from an Arapaho word meaning earthborn spirit.

The Area

Something remarkable awaits you when you visit Vedauwoo that most American of climbing areas. Here, massive multi-colored blocks of strangely shaped, Precambrian granite tower above the brush covered plains of southeastern Wyoming. This high oasis is filled with reflective beaver ponds and sturdy stands of pine and aspen. Red tailed hawks, golden eagles, and ravens soar in the vaulted blue dome that envelopes the high plains of the American West. These gliding birds monitor ground squirrels, marmots, antelope, coyote, and ermine, as well as artifacts like climbers, cowboys, and grazing cattle. From the tops of the crags you can look south for over a hundred miles to the Continental Divide and see the apex of the northern Rockies, the Diamond of Longs Peak. Vedauwoo is blessed with climbs at all levels of difficulty and is a great place for the beginning leader, since route finding and protection are usually straightforward, the rock is solid, and descents lack adventure and rubble. The experienced leader will also be challenged since there are 5.13 routes as diverse as offwidths (yes!) and bolt protected faces. There is lots of climbing for the rest of us, and new route potential still abounds even at moderate levels of difficulty.

The rock at Vedauwoo is a rough granite with many inclusions and imparts a very high coefficient of friction whether wanted or not. This makes for solid jams in cracks (tape!) and for very steep slab climbing. In fact, some of the new slab routes are so steep they give the impression of being overhanging. Climbers from other areas are amazed at first by the steepness of the slab routes. The amazement soon gives way to joy as they climb with confidence smooth looking faces that even close to the cliff look impossible. Above all, Vedauwoo is known for its many crack climbs which go from finger nails to chimney (an early guidebook was simply called *Crack Country*). Most Vedauwoo climbs are one pitch with a moderate number of two pitch climbs. Some longer routes can be strung together, especially in the Central Area. A sustained level of difficulty is a predominant characteristic of Vedauwoo climbs. As John Harlin wrote, "Vedauwoo could be a lost and unheralded twin of ...Joshua Tree."

LOCATION AND SEASON

V edauwoo lies 16 miles east of Laramie, Wyoming on the north side of I-80, a major east-west, transcontinental highway. See inside back cover. This is 140 miles from Denver via I-25 and I-80. State Highway 210 (Happy Jack Road) goes from Cheyenne to just east of Laramie. For the most part, it runs parallel to and north of I-80. Some climbing and camping facilities adjoin Happy Jack Road. The Vedauwoo Turnoff is Exit 329 on I-80. The elevation at Vedauwoo is a little more than 8,000 feet. Since the crags have no preferred direction, you can climb in the sun or shade as conditions dictate. In theory there is climbing year round. While that may be true for locals who can race out in the middle of a sunny winter day, visitors will find that reliable conditions occur between May and October. Traditionalists will note that climbing before Easter or Passover is unlikely but the season is usually in full swing by Pentecost. Climbing in the summer and early fall is incredibly pleasant. Vedauwoo is a frequent refuge from those seeking relief from the heat, rain, and insects that prevail in many other areas of North America during the summer months. However, the wind season can be a bit trying. It usually starts in early January and lasts until late December. As is the case with other Rocky Mountain areas, summer days tend to be clear and sunny, the nights cool, while unexpected thunderstorms, often accompanied by hail, can appear at any time but are most frequent in the late afternoon.

CAMPING AND ACCOMMODATIONS

Vedauwoo (officially, the name is Vedauwoo Recreational Area) is in the Medicine Bow National Forest. Free camping is allowed everywhere except where it is explicitly prohibited. There is also a fee campground having 12 sites near the Central Area. It has the so-called "primitive facilities": parking sites, water, picnic tables, grills, and outhouses but no showers. There are three other National Forest Service Campgrounds with primitive facilities within seven miles of Vedauwoo: Tie City (25 sites), Yellow Pine (19 sites), and Pole Creek (18 sites). Proceed six miles west along I-80 from the Vedauwoo turnoff, and exit at The Summit State Rest Area (Lincoln Monument). Go north on Route 703 for about a mile and then turn east on Route 722 which will lead to the three campgrounds. Curt Gowdy State Park (280 sites), which also has primitive facilities, is located on the south side of Happy Jack road about seven miles from Vedauwoo. Proceed to the north side of Vedauwoo where Route 700 intersects Happy Jack Road. Then go east for six miles. If you are coming from the east, the campground is approximately 23 miles west of Cheyenne along the Happy Jack Road.

All the usual amenities are available in Laramie where motel and restaurant prices are modest by national standards. There are two commercial campgrounds in Laramie: KOA, 1171 Baker St. [307-742-4177] and Riverside, I-80 &

Curtis [307-721-7405]. General tourist information can be obtained from the Albany County Tourist Board, 800 S. Third St., Laramie WY 82070 [307-745-7339 or 800-445-5303]. Jeffrey's and its informal annex, Jeffrey's II, provide good food in a pleasant ambiance. Imbibing at Coal Creek Coffee House will get you moving in the morning. Tim's Outdoor Store [412 Grand Ave., Laramie, (307)745-8775] and Bradley Mountain Wear [213 South First St., Laramie, (307)742-9490] carry a full line of climbing supplies. A new route list is maintained at Tim's Store.

ETHICS

Vedauwoo follows what has become the North American Standard Ethic. Don't bolt when natural protection is available. Don't bolt anywhere near a crack. Be modest in the use of bolts (Vedauwoo is *not* a bolt a meter area!), and make them camouflaged. Don't leave slings on the cliffs. Never chip holds. Don't retrobolt other people's routes. Don't spook grazing cattle (keep your dogs under control-- they could be shot). Remove litter that you come across, and don't be a slob. Gardening of routes is acceptable, but the chopping of trees is unacceptable. Visitors should consult with local climbers before placing bolts, since the line you're contemplating may have been climbed earlier without such hardware. In fact, before you claim a line as a first ascent, check with Bob Scarpelli. He probably climbed it in tennis shoes years ago. Adhere to the Access Fund Guidelines given elsewhere in this book. If you don't follow these simple rules, may your delinquent grandchildren piss on your pauper's grave.

Note this carefully: the Forest Service has been reviewing climbing activities at Vedauwoo. Thus far they have been reasonable and responsive to inputs from the climbing community. The Forest Service wishes to emphasize that they recognize technical climbing as a legitimate and historical use of National Forest Lands, but it is not an activity they endorse or for which they are responsible. A recent concern of the Forest Service has been a number of accidents involving drunken "climbers". Predominately, these have been visitors who come to Vedauwoo to party. Inspired by the cliffs and real climbers and with their inhibitions weakened, they decide to take to the rocks. Unfortunately, this has a negative impact, not only upon the inebriated individuals who fall while attempting to get up a route, but also on the reputation of the entire climbing community. Whatever you do, don't climb if you've been drinking or taking any other performance impairing, psychoactive substances whether physician prescribed or self selected. If you've enjoyed your visit here, let the Forest Service know about it. Most importantly, help maintain the positive relationship with the Forest Service by being a good citizen or a good tourist when you visit here.

Figure 1.1 Done a first ascent? Check with Bob Scarpelli. He probably did it years ago ... in tennis shoes! Photo courtesy of Piana/Cowboyography.

IMPORTANT ADDRESSES AND TELEPHONE NUMBERS

Call 911 in case of an emergency. There may be a cellular telephone at Campsite No. 1, if the campground host is in residence. Otherwise, the nearest public telephone is at the Summit State Rest Area (Lincoln Monument) on the north side of I-80 and six miles west of the Vedauwoo turnoff. Search and rescue services are handled by a Sheriff's Posse from the Albany County Sheriff's Office out of Laramie. When telephoning, it will speed the rescue if you locate precisely where the accident occurred. Name the crag and on what side of the formation help is needed. Twenty four hour emergency medical care can be obtained at Ivinson Memorial Hospital in Laramie. The hospital has available full orthopedic services and resources for outdoor related medical problems.

Emergency: Call 911. Always call this number for Sheriff or Hospital Emergency Service.

Sheriff's Office, Albany County (Supervises Search and Rescue)
525 Grand Ave.
Laramie WY 82070
Telephone: (307) 721-2526

Forest Service, U.S. Dept. of Agriculture
Laramie Ranger District
Medicine Bow National Forest
2468 Jackson St.
Laramie WY 82070-6535
Telephone: (307) 745-8971

Ivinson Memorial Hospital
255 N. 30th St.
Laramie WY 82070
Telephone: (307) 742-2141, Ext. 222 for Emergency Room

COMPASSES, WATCH FACES AND MAPS

The cliffs have no preferred directions, and often a structure such as a jutting flange will have a direction different than the main line of the cliff face. This presents difficulties in describing a climb, since it's easy to get the words jumbled when, say, the climb being described faces east even though the cliff on which the climb occurs faces southwest. The simplest solution to this problem, and the one which allows for the minimal number of words, is simply to give the compass direction of the climb. Most crag climbers don't carry compasses. However, they are inexpensive, simple to use and will make it easier to follow the directions in the guide. We often employ numerical compass directions in which N is 0°, E is 90°, S is 180°, and W is 270°. When we say a cliff faces 270° or is oriented to 270°, we mean: if you are standing with your back to the cliff, then your nose will be pointing towards 270°, that is, due west. More technically, 270° is the compass direction that an arrow will face if it points straight out from the cliff. We always give the compass direction we have measured. We have not corrected for magnetic declination. Highway I-80 runs along a southeast to northwest axis in the vicinity of Vedauwoo. This often causes visitors' instinctive sense of direction to be in error, since it seems the highway should go east to west.

We use watch face descriptions for pointing out features en route. For example, we may write, "...after the last bolt look for a thin crack at 2:00." Here "2:00" is short for "two o'clock." In watch face directions, 12:00 is always straight ahead, 3:00 is to the right, 6:00 is to the rear, and 9:00 is to the left. Thus, 1:30 is a direction half way between straight ahead and due right.

The two U.S. Department of the Interior Geological Survey Maps that cover the areas described in this book are: *Sherman Mountains East Quadrangle, Wyoming* and *Sherman Mountains West Quadrangle, Wyoming*. The Forest Service Map that covers the entire Medicine Bow National Forest is: *National Forest and Grassland Visitor Maps, Medicine Bow (Wyoming)*. This map as well as a *Free Visitor Guide to Medicine Bow National Forest* may be obtained from the Forest Service at the address given above.

RATINGS, SAFETY, AND GEAR

We use the standard *Yosemite decimal system* that starts at 5.0. From 5.7 to 5.9 we may add a plus or minus, for example, 5.7+ means the route is at the high end of difficulty for the range. The suffices a, b, c, and d are attached to ratings 5.10 and higher in accordance with standard practice. The 5. at the front of the ratings carries no useful information but has become ingrained by habit. We have dropped it in the listing of the climbs. For example, a route will be listed as **23. My Dog 8+**. This means route 23 is named *My Dog* and its rating is 5.8+. When speaking people often use the preliminary "5." in referring to routes less than 5.10 in difficulty and drop it for routes 5.10 or harder. Thus, common spoken usage is, "I made a desperate 5.8 hand jam and then a 13b mantle." We mostly follow that practice in the descriptive portions of the text employing what sounds right. The Yosemite rating system is not logical, since it has grown organically and historically rather than being modified by design as the nature of climbing has changed. If we had the courage of our convictions, we would have used the Australian rating system which is simple and logical. See the article by Randy Vogel, *Rating Game Part IV*, in the Bibliography for a thorough analysis of rating a climb.

SYMBOLS
USED IN GRAPHICS

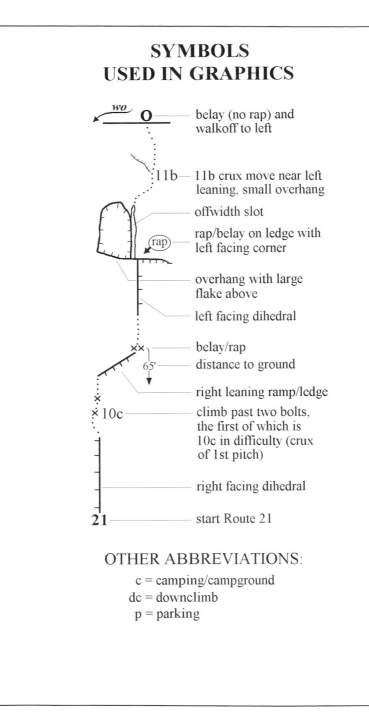

belay (no rap) and
walkoff to left

11b crux move near left
leaning, small overhang

offwidth slot

rap/belay on ledge with
left facing corner

overhang with large
flake above

left facing dihedral

belay/rap

distance to ground

right leaning ramp/ledge

climb past two bolts,
the first of which is
10c in difficulty (crux
of 1st pitch)

right facing dihedral

start Route 21

OTHER ABBREVIATIONS:

c = camping/campground
dc = downclimb
p = parking

Figure 1.2

Jim Erickson in *Rocky Heights* introduced a system of ratings of R and X, to which PG was added later, to indicate the objective danger on a route. It's a good system and applied perfectly to the Boulder area that Erickson was writing about. We have not used it since, in general, Vedauwoo does not have much rotten rock and most routes protect fairly well. If a route has objective dangers associated with it, such as a long runout or poor protection, we attempt to mention that specifically in the text. However, you **cannot assume** that the route protects well or lacks objective dangers just because we do not mention such dangers. Physical condition, technical ability, judgment, and weather as well as other factors which cannot be foreseen by the authors will influence the degree of danger for a given climber on specific route on a given day. Further, the route itself can change intrinsically as holds break off or rock fractures occur because of thawing and freezing or other natural events. Also, the variable and informal nature of our information sources can lead to conclusions at variance with the actual nature of the route. There is no substitute for your own judgment and experience.

For years Vedauwoo has had the reputation of stiff ratings. This has not been true for the most part. Ratings from 5.0 to 5.5 and for 5.10+ and above have generally corresponded to national and rational standards. Ratings of climbs between 5.6 and 5.10 generated the most controversy. Most such routes were accurately rated, but maybe some 20% were off even compared to other Vedauwoo climbs. Accuracy is the only standard for a rating. However, a rating can be influenced by such extraneous factors as insecure status, faulty ego structure, group think, xenophobic bigotry, outmoded standards, obsequious deference to the first ascensionist, and compulsive repetition of a route. Also, many of the routes in question are fist to offwidth cracks. Modern climbers trained on plastic walls or bolt protected faces find such routes puzzling. Having assumed they were 5.11 climbers, they are incensed when they find that can't redpoint a 5.6. However, inexperience is not an appropriate guide in rating a climb. In the course of writing this book, we have reclimbed several of the routes with controversial ratings. We have left most unchanged, while others have been increased from a half to one and half in degree of difficulty and a few lowered in rating. We have also taken into account the difficulty of placing protection when rating a route. A route that would be 5.9 if bolt protected can reasonably be rated 5.10a when the skill and effort to place natural protection are factored into the rating. As is the North American custom, the rating for a route corresponds in most instances to the hardest single move, but there are exceptions. For example, if the hardest move is essentially a boulder problem getting started, it might not work its way into the grade. Some climbs are graded as more difficult because of their very sustained nature. Assigning ratings has proved to be one of the most enjoyable tasks in writing this book -- at last in print, the truth according to us.

We always use *free climb* in this book in the sense of redpoint. A route is climbed *redpoint* if none of the equipment is used to overcome the effects of gravity, equipment is used only for safety, and all movable protection gear is placed on lead. More simply, the climber doesn't weight the gear or rope and sets the gear as he climbs. For purposes of this definition it doesn't matter if the route was previously attempted in any style. As Kurt Albert, the inventor of the redpoint concept has stated, "Redpoint is a definition; it is not a statement of morality." However, a moral issue is raised if you imply you redpointed the route but actually climbed it in another style. A *pinkpoint* is an ascent in which gear, such as quick draws or camming devices, are placed prior to the ascent but otherwise meets the standards for redpoint. An intermediate version between redpoint and pinkpoint is a *strict yo-yo*. If the climber falls or otherwise weights the gear, he is lowered to the ground or a safe rest stance. He pulls the rope through the weighted piece to avoid having a top rope and starts climbing again. The ascent, except for this variance, meets the standards of redpoint. Yo-yo is perhaps the most workable definition of free climbing for multipitch routes. Occasionally, it is called brownpoint.

We often mention getting from one point to another by "scrambling" or by "third classing." *Scrambling* means hiking with occasional rock climbing moves. *Third classing* means easy technical climbing where a rope is not usually used. The term *downclimbing* means descending in third class style. However, the decision whether or not to use a rope in these situations is yours and not that of a guidebook author. Physical condition, technical ability, judgment, and weather as well as other factors which cannot be foreseen by the authors will influence whether or not a rope should be used in a given circumstance. As is the case with rappelling, some well known, leading climber is seriously injured or killed each year while third classing on easy rock. **When in doubt, rope up!**

Rappelling is always a source of danger, since the climber is totally dependent upon his gear. We usually indicate when a rappel requires more than one rope, that is, the rappel is longer than 80 feet, or when it comes close to that length. However, it's likely that we have not so described all such rappels given the informal and variable sources of our information. Each climber is responsible for employing safe rappel techniques. In particular, he or she has full responsibility to be prepared for the rappel rope not touching the ground and for checking the structural integrity of the rappel anchors.

Fig. 1.2 shows the conventions and symbols used in the graphics. Please note that the indication of the number of pitches on a route and the locations of belay stations are suggestive and not definitive. Climbers with different skill levels or different temperaments will choose to have fewer or more pitches on a route than those listed in the text. Weather conditions, fatigue, route finding, inadequate gear, and other conditions not foreseen or foreseeable by the authors may dictate belaying at places other than those suggested.

A generic rack for a Vedauwoo crack climb about which you have no previous knowledge would include one of everything from RP's to large stoppers and a full set of Friends. For larger cracks such as fists or offwidths, the #4 Camalot is an extremely useful piece as it is easy to set and covers a wide range of widths. It can make the difference between backing off a climb or flashing it. For cracks beyond fists, #2-#4 Big Bros are very useful. Big Dudes are easier to set than Big Bros but generally have a fairly small range in which they hold securely. A generic half rack is the full standard rack with every other piece removed. We sometimes, but not always, mention if a doubling up of certain gear is desirable. We assume the reader will use common sense. For example, if you're staring at a long finger crack, you might need some extra small pieces even if nothing is mentioned in the text. Sturdy, long pants and long sleeved shirts are advisable for the wider cracks, and knee pads can be a real comfort in chimneys. The best type is the Neoprene wrap arounds since they stay in position. Knee pads are sometimes helpful on offwidths but often times decrease the sensitivity needed to set a good knee jam.

GETTING ORIENTED

Since the cliffs at Vedauwoo have no preferred direction, the first time visitor may find it confusing to locate them. A little time spent on orientation at the beginning will make it a lot easier to find your way around. A neat way to get a general survey is to pick out the crags (binoculars helpful) as you drive along Route 700. (n.b., *Vedauwoo Turnoff* refers to Exit 329 on I-80 which leads to National Forest Route 700). You will get an especially good overview of the great horseshoe shaped massif forming Central Vedauwoo (Fig. 1.4) as well as many outlying formations (Fig. 1.3). Most of the crags on the massif, from Holy Saturday on the west end to Old Easy on the east end, will be visible on your tour. Mileage's refer to distances from the cattle guard at the beginning of Route 700.

- **0.0 miles.** The outlying Poland Hill is visible to the left (north) about a half mile away. At 10:30 (northeast) *Straight and Narrow* dihedral can be seen high atop Turtle Rock. Hassler's Hatbox formation is at 11:00 high up on the horizon.

- **0.4 miles**. A dome shaped structure becomes visible at the north end of Poland Hill. It's often likened to a rat brain with *Fantasia* forming the longitudinal fissure while *Petit Crapon* forms the Sylvian fissure. The Blair area is 2.3

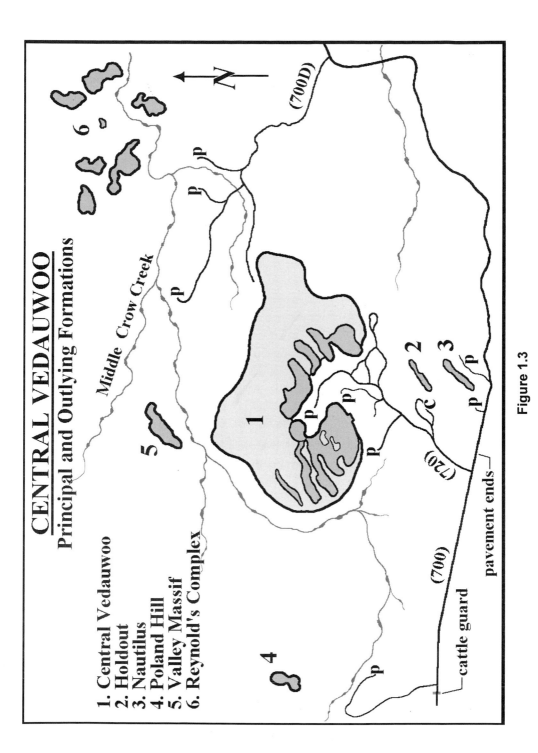

Figure 1.3

miles away at 09:00 (northeast). On the left is Blair I and on the right is the Heap. With binoculars you can see the *SpectreMan* dihedral on the right edge of the Heap.

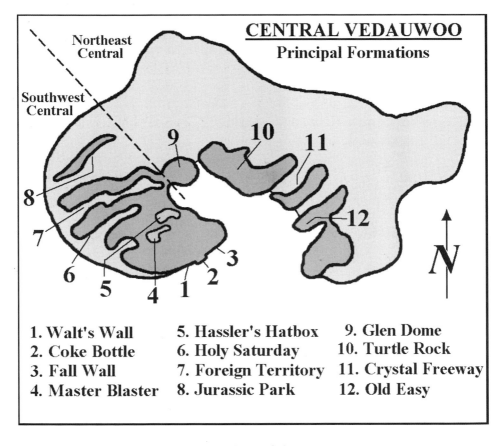

1. Walt's Wall
2. Coke Bottle
3. Fall Wall
4. Master Blaster
5. Hassler's Hatbox
6. Holy Saturday
7. Foreign Territory
8. Jurassic Park
9. Glen Dome
10. Turtle Rock
11. Crystal Freeway
12. Old Easy

Figure 1.4

- **0.45 miles.** Looking to the left through a notch in the hills you can see the southwest side of Valley Massif on whose far right side is the *Hooker* dihedral.

- **0.8 miles.** The overhanging southeast face of Holy Saturday, split down the middle by *Hide-A-Way Chimney*, is visible at 09:00. Now look to 10:30 and the right side of a mass covered with broken rocks. You will see the left face of the Coke Bottle dihedral with the left leaning crack, *Horn's Mother,* splitting the face. *Ruffis,* a crescent shaped crack, can be seen on the right side of Hassler's Hatbox. Old Easy is to the right at 11:00. Friction Tower is between Old Easy and the Coke Bottle. The northwest side of Holdout, with a spike of rock on its top, is farther to the right across a gap. Nautilus is straight ahead. Its high point is the Parabolic Slab which can be seen near the right end of Nautilus.

- **1.05 miles.** Turtle Rock reappears between the Coke Bottle and Friction Tower.

- **1.15 miles.** Go left (Route 720) towards the Central Area. The junction of Routes 700 and 720 is referred to as the Central Area Turnoff. Shortly after the turn you can see *Edwards' Crack* splitting the face that is left of the Coke Bottle. Hassler's Hatbox sits high above this face and about 100 yards in back of it. On the left side of the Hatbox is a huge roof along whose right side is *Lucille.*

- **1.35 miles.** The campground turnoff is on the right.

- **1.5 miles.** The Master Blaster area is visible below the Lucille Roof. *Master Blaster* starts along a right facing dihedral and continues on a right leaning crack through the upper wall.

- **1.6 miles.** Stop at the pull out on the left side of the road for an excellent, straight on view of the Walt's Wall Area. Two lines are obvious: *Edwards' Crack* on the left and *Bell Crack* which splits the Coke Bottle. Moving on, bear left at the fork in the road.

- **1.7 miles.** At this juncture you can turn left for the upper parking lot or bear left for Robber's Roost Road. Choose Robber's Roost Road.

- **1.9 miles.** *MRC* on Old Easy is on the right above some immense boulders.

- **2.1 miles.** The parking lot at the end of the road. *Water Streak* on Glen Dome is straight ahead (west). Crystal Freeway is at 05:00 (northeast) and Turtle Rock is at 03:00 (northwest). At 10:00 (southwest) is the right end of Hassler's Hatbox under whose roof is the exit for *Journey To Coramonde*.

Now drive back to the upper parking lot. The slabs straight ahead (i.e., to the right of the Coke Bottle) are the Fall Wall and Cold Finger areas. Turning around and looking south you will see the Northwest Side of Holdout. You should be able to discern a prominent right leaning diagonal line, *Currey's Diagonal*. Go back to Route 700 and turn left (southeast) heading towards Nautilus. Looking up towards Nautilus you can see the steep, flat southwest face of the Ted's Trot Block which contains *Drunken Redneck Rappelers*. The crack to the left is *Finally*. Continuing along the road for another half mile, you will get a panoramic view of the Southeast Side of Nautilus. Prominent features to look for along the way are the back side of the Parabolic Slab and below it *Flying Buttress* and a bit to the right *Piton Perch*. Near the right end of Nautilus you can make out the apse sheltering *Friday the 13th*. Near the very right end, a huge shield of rock stands in front of the main massif. *Middle Parallel Space* is on the left side of the shield. This concludes your 50¢ tour of Vedauwoo.

BIBLIOGRAPHY

We list here all the articles and books that we are aware of concerning climbing at Vedauwoo as well as a few items of general interest.

1. Anderson, Jay. *Lucille,* **Rock & Ice**, No. 44, July 1991, pp. 34-37.

2. Blackstone, D.L., Jr. *Traveler's Guide To The Geology Of Wyoming, Bulletin No. 67, 2nd printing (corrected*), 130 pages, Geological Survey of Wyoming, P.O. Box 3008, University Station, Laramie WY 82071, 1988 (corrected 1992).

3. Blunk, Scott. *Basecamp Report, Wyoming,* **Climbing**, No. 115, August 1989, pp. 34-35.

4. Blunk, Scott. *Basecamp Report, Wyoming,* **Climbing**, No. 119, April 1990, pp. 52-53.

5. Bonney, Orin H. and Bonney, Lorraine G. *Guide To The Wyoming Mountains and Wilderness Areas*, 3rd ed., 701 pages, Swallow Press, Chicago, 1977.

6. Erickson, Jim. *Rocky Heights, -- A Guide to Boulder Free Climbs,* 280 pages, self published, Boulder CO, 1980.

7. Garson, John; Kopischka, Layne; and Pousch, Gary, *Crack Country--A Climbing Guide To Vedauwoo*, 48 pages, self-published, Laramie WY, 1977.

8. Glass, Gary B. and Blackstone, D. L., Jr. *Geology of Wyoming*, 12 pages, Information Pamphlet No. 2, Geological Survey of Wyoming, P.O. Box 3008, University Station, Laramie WY 82071, 1992.

9. Halfpenny, Jim. *A Climber's Guide To Southeastern Wyoming*, 77 pages, self-published, Laramie WY, 1972.

10. Harlin, John, III. *The Climber's Guide To North America: Rocky Mountain Rock Climbs*, 395 pages, Chockstone Press, Denver, 1985.

11. Harper, Skip and Kelman, Rob. *Guide to Greater Vedauwoo*, **Rock & Ice**, No. 61, May 1994, pp. 77-82.

12. Hunger, Bill. *The Hiker's Guide To Wyoming*, 222 pages, Falcon Press, Helena MT, 1992.

13. Kelman, Robert. Book Review: *Cracks Unlimited* by Layne Kopischka, **Climbing**, No. 104, October 1987, pp. 123-125.

14. Kopischka, Layne. *Crack Country Revisited*, 66 pages, self-published, Laramie WY, 1982.

15. Kopischka, Layne. *Cracks Unlimited*, 77 pages, self-published, Laramie WY, 1987.

16. Kopischka, Layne. *Vedauwoo Rock--A Climbing Guide To Vedauwoo*, 76 pages, self-published, Laramie WY, 1992.

17. Mathiesen, Jan and Halfpenny, Jim. *Vedauwoo Climbing*, 11 pages, self-published, Laramie WY, 1966.

18. Piana, Paul. *Vedauwoo*, **Climbing**, No. 72, May 1982, pp. 24-27.

19. Piana, Paul. *Basecamp Report, Wyoming*, **Climbing**, No. 75, December 1982, pp. 9-10.

20. Piana, Paul. *Basecamp Report, Wyoming*, **Climbing**, No. 84, June 1984, pp. 11-12.

21. Piana, Paul. *Basecamp Report, Wyoming*, **Climbing**, No. 89, April 1985, pp. 11-12

16

22. Piana, Paul. *Vedauwoo, **Climbing**, No. 122, October 1990, pp. 56-58.

23. Prichard, Nancy. *Mommas, Don't Let Your Cowboys Grow Up To Be Climbers,* **Rock & Ice**, No. 44, July 1991, pp. 48-51.

24. Skinner, Todd. *Earthborn Spirit,* **Rock & Ice**, No. 44, July 1991, pp. 28-33.

25. Snoke, Arthur W., Steidtman, James R., and Roberst, Sheila M. *Geology of Wyoming, Geological Survey of Wyoming Memoir No. 5,* 938 pages, Geological Survey of Wyoming, P.O. Box 3008, University Station, Laramie WY 82071, 1993.

26. Sublett, Jerry., Garson, John., and Zimmerman, Roger., *Vedauwoo Climbs,* 40 pages, self-published, Laramie WY 1972.

27. Vogel, Randy. *The American Guidebook, Part II. The Trouble With Guidebooks,* **Climbing**, No. 99, December 1986, p.73.

28. Vogel, Randy. *The American Guidebook, Part IV. The Rating Game -- Stuttering In Tongues,* **Climbing**, No. 101, April 1987, pp. 98-101.

29. Vogel, Randy. *The American Guidebook, Part V. Wyoming Guidebooks,* **Climbing**, No. 102, June 1987, p. 112.

30. Vogler, Romain. Les Étas-Unis les Plus Belles Escalades, Ch. Vedauwoo, pp. 65-67, Publ. De Noël, Paris, 1984.

31. Webster, Ed. Book Reviews, **Climbing**, No. 84, June 1984, pp. 60-61.

2. SUGGESTED ROUTES

A star system is not used to rate climbs, since it's not all that useful at Vedauwoo. In many other areas, climbs vary from the sublime to the awful within the space of a few feet, and often it is difficult to make this distinction just by examining the route from the ground. Most climbs at Vedauwoo are good and, in any case, tend to be what they look like. We do mention in the text those climbs that we regard as outstanding and those that are dreadful. Also, our experience with books that do use the star system has been that many good routes are left unstarred. Further, many climbers will miss interesting experiences by doing only classical warhorses as important aspects of the climbing experience are only savored on bad routes. In any event, selecting climbs for quality is very subjective and depends as much on current fashion as on inherent quality. For example, *October Light* and *Max Factor* are two excellent, easily accessible routes of comparable difficulty and quality on the Nautilus. Yet, one is a popular climb and the other is seldom attempted.

We present a list of good climbs from 5.0 through 5.11 that provide an overall sampling of Vedauwoo and which should assist first time visitors in getting a sense of the crags and climbing available. This list is not restricted to the best climbs, and, in fact, some fine climbs that are highly recommended in the text are not listed here. Our purpose is not to encourage the mobbing of a few, excellent, easily accessible routes. In general, if two very good climbs are located close to each other, we only list one of them. A route that is the outstanding example at its rating on a crag is more likely to be listed than another climb of comparable or better quality which is located near several other similar climbs. We also have chosen the routes so as to emphasize different types of climbing.

We have not presumed to suggest routes from among the 34 climbs in the 5.12 to 5.13 range. Practically all of these are good routes, and they are very distinct and have unique histories. Those who climb at this level should have little trouble finding routes to their liking which will offer them really fine climbing.

Suggested Routes

5.0 to 5.5

Cornelius
Drain Pipe
Etude for the Right Hand
Foolishness
Glenn's First Name

Hide-A-Way Chimney
Right Parallel Space
Soft Touch
Southwest Friction
Sunny Day

5.6

Becker
Bill Steal
Bushwhack
Cave Crack
Horticulture

Kim
Maiden
Moor Crossing
Piton Perch
Stinkzig

5.7

Big House
Edwards' Crack
Hassler's Hatbox Route
Kitchen's Delight (Croissant Start)
Mother #1

MRC Left
Screw
Sugar Crack
T-M Chimney
Upper Slot

5.8

Baobab Tree
Cat's Cradle
Flake
Oslund's Delight
Satterfield's Crack

Sore-O-Pod
Straight and Narrow
Strawberry Jam
Tea Grinder
Tombstone Crack

5.9

Climb and Punishment
Fantasia
Grunt Layback
Intimidation
Jet Stream
Middle Parallel Space

MRC Direct/Straight Edge
Plumb Line
Quits
Serpentine
Slot-A-Saurus
Water Streak II

5.10a/b

Arete Aready
Beef Eater
Citadel Crack
Currey's Diagonal
Fall Wall Route
Flying Buttress

Mainstreet
Pooh Corner
S.S. Maywood
Skull
Thing of Beauty
Victory of Defeat

5.10c/d

Atherolichenous Plaque
Date With a Dike
Grand Traverse
Hooker
Japan Club
Left Torpedo Tube

Lichen Lung
Master Blaster
Medium Cool
Moonrise Variation
Penis Dimension
Ultra Violets

5.11a/b

Blade Runner
Boardwalk
Ghost Dance
Good-bye White Opel
Granite Stairway
Hung Like a Horse

Orange Christmas
Piece of Dirt
Rainbow in the Dark
Ruffis
Spider God
What the French Girl Said

5.11c/d

Arch Stanton
Deadman's Glove
Eleven Cent Moon
Friday the 13th
Light From Blue Horses
London Calling

Moonsault
Muscle and Fitness
Soft Parade
SpectreMan
Superb Arete
Whaling on Napalm

3. SOUTHWEST CENTRAL

S|outhwest Central is that part of the great horseshoe forming the Central Mas-
sif that lies to the southwest of Robbers' Roost Road. It encompasses Walt's
Wall Area, The Coke Bottle, Fall Wall and Cold Finger Areas, Master Blaster
Area, Hassler's Hatbox, Holy Saturday, Foreign Territory, and Jurassic Park (Fig.
1.4). The sector from Walt's Wall to Fall Wall (Figs. 3.1-3.9) is the most popular
area at Vedauwoo for it is easily accessible and has many classic routes. This is
both a blessing and a curse as many popular routes become overcrowded. De-
spair not! Many other fine routes are available even in this one area, let alone in
the many other rocky eminences at Vedauwoo. With so much fine, easily accessible rock to climb there is no need to wait in line (unless that is what you enjoy).

WALT'S WALL AREA

Walt's Wall (Fig. 3.1) was one of the original climbing areas. Established routes
go back to the 1940's. Thus, it contains many fine, moderate climbs as well as
more demanding modern test pieces as a new generation of climbers started ex-
ploring its supposedly unclimbable faces in the 1980's. You can descend by rappel from the rappel stations atop *Walt's Wall Route* or *Fourth of July Crack*.
Beginners are advised to use 2 ropes for this last rappel, otherwise some 3rd
class scrambling will be required. There is also a walkoff: go straight ahead from
the end of *Walt's Wall Route* for 50 yards, veer right (northeast) to an obvious
drainage, and follow it down to Robber's Roost Road. Use the following routes for
orientation: *Edwards' Crack, Satterfield's Crack, Bell Crack, Fallout, 5.11 Crack,*
and *E.O. Lieback.*

1.   Five Sleazy Creases 9   Start about 15 yards left of *Foolishness* on the ex-
treme left shoulder of Walt's Wall Area. Climb up a slab cut by 5 grooves of which
the middle groove is the deepest.

2.   Tourist Trap 4   The trap is this: if you climb the route, you must either downclimb it or choose a more difficult route to exit. Start on a lower shelf 40 yards left
of *Edwards' Crack*. Climb a right leaning ramp that forms at places an offwidth
crack with the main wall. Continue to the start of the final pitch of *Edwards' Crack*.

3.   Foolishness 4   Crowded on *Walt's Wall Route*? Then get real with this fine,
serious climb featuring wide cracks and slab. Start on the left diagonaling slab 8
yards right of the start of *Tourist Trap*. Climb along a dihedral whose right side is
a vertical wall. After 20 feet join up with *Tourist Trap*. At this point turn right up the
ramp until near its middle where there is another left leaning ramp with a dihedral
corner formed by a vertical wall. Belay here. Climb the left leaning ramp, and be-

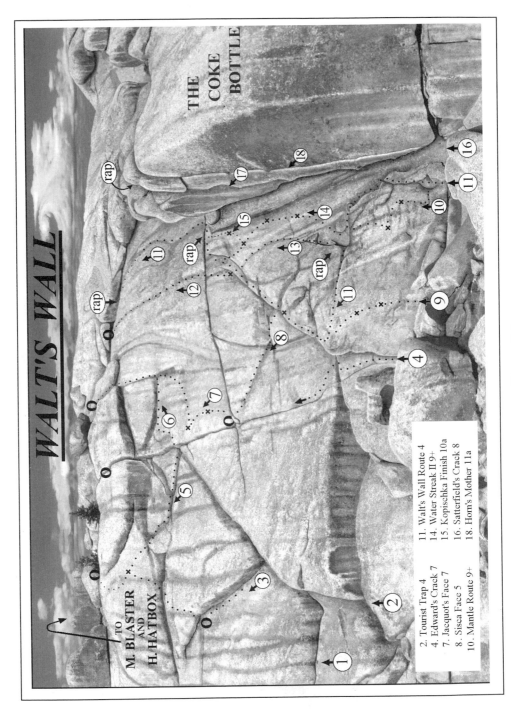

WALT'S WALL

THE COKE BOTTLE

TO
M. BLASTER
AND
H. HATBOX

2. Tourist Trap 4
4. Edward's Crack 7
7. Jacquot's Face 7
8. Sisca Face 5
10. Mantle Route 9+
11. Walt's Wall Route 4
14. Water Streak II 9+
15. Kopischka Finish 10a
16. Satterfield's Crack 8
18. Horn's Mother 11a

Figure 3.1

lay just before it ends. Head right and climb two short headwalls and an exposed face moving past the bolt on *Edward's' Crack, Left Exit.*

4. Edwards' Crack 7- Classic. You can't miss this 120 foot crack which splits Walt's Wall from the base through its roof exit. Start by a right leaning dihedral and struggle up for about 15 feet (7) to a left slanting hand crack. Follow it across a gap to a face, traverse left into the main crack, and belay at the middle ledge. Push straight through the wide crack on the headwall (7). The traditional rating for this climb is 5.6. Except for the 2 isolated moves of 5.7 most of the climbing is 5.5.

5. Edwards' Crack, Left Exit 4 Belay on the little shelf below the final headwall of *Edwards' Crack*. Traverse left along the shelf for about 15 feet, and then move up slanting left on a neat friction face past a bolt to the top. Very nice, very exposed.

6. Edwards' Crack, Right Exit 5 Same start as the preceding climb. Traverse out right along the final headwall until encountering a dihedral. Climb the crack on the wall forming the right face of the dihedral. Very nice, very funky.

7. Jacquot's Face 7 This is an alternate right exit to *Edwards' Crack*. From the belay ledge at the end of the first pitch of *Edwards' Crack*, walk right 12 feet until below a bolt. Climb to it, angle left to another bolt, slant up right to a left facing dihedral, and finish by joining *Edwards' Crack, Right Exit.*

8. Sisca Face 5 Combining this route with the start of *Edwards' Crack* and finishing with *Jacquot's Face* provides a moderate way to the top of Walt's Wall while avoiding most of *Walt's Wall Route* and *Edwards' Crack* which are often crowded. Climb the first 10 feet of *Edwards' Crack*, and continue to the right up a gully. When feasible, head left up the face (no protection) to a small ledge. Continue left until the belay stance for *Edwards' Crack*.

9. Friction Slide 8 Start atop a flake 12 yards left of *Walt's Wall Route,* and climb a shallow trough passing two bolts on the way to the first ledge in *Walt's Wall Route*. (This is an ancient solo by Mike Covington which was recently bolted.)

10. Mantle Route 9+ This is a good toprope problem but leaves something to be desired as a lead, since the first effective protection comes 40 feet off the deck and *after* the crux. It serves as an example of how not to bolt a route. Climb the start of *Walt's Wall Route* to the little ledge. It's possible to place some gear in the cracks on the right. Traverse left 10 feet, climb to a bolt, and traverse left to the next bolt followed by easy climbing to the ledge. (Most of this route was probably done by 1965 and called *Koedt's Route.* It made a more direct start to the left,

Figure 3.2 *Edwards' Crack (7-)* **is a must do route. A climber is shown at the first crux of this famous climb.**

had a bolt lower down and a move of aid near the start. It is unfortunate that this version was not pushed to become a free climb, since it is a more natural line than *Mantle Route.*)

11. Walt's Wall Route 4 Beginner's classic. Start 4 yards to the left of the bulging dihedral on the right. Surmount a flake, climb the cracks straight above or, more interestingly, move right a few feet and mantle on a corbel. Then veering left, climb the wide crack (protection) or out on the face (no protection) to a sizable ledge on which there are belay bolts on the left. Clip into the bolts but continue to the end of the ledge where a gear belay may be set up. This avoids interference with the traffic that gathers near the bolts and lessens rope drag on the next pitch. Climb the right leaning ramp past a couple of bolts and move right to an I-bolt belay. The last pitch starts a couple of feet further right, ascends the face to a flake (medium sized protection) and then up to another I-bolt.

12. Jake's Variation 5 Traverse left for 10 feet from the second belay stance on *Walt's Wall Route* from whence a bolt can be seen on the wall. Climb past the bolt en route to a second bolt and the belay atop *Walt's Wall Route.*

13. 5.7 Cracks 7 Belay at the bolts on the first pitch of *Walt's Wall Route.* Then climb up the crack flake structure to the right and follow the line of least resistance as it arches left to join the ramp on the second pitch of *Walt's Wall Route.* Nice climb but skimpy protection. Mostly small pieces.

14. Water Streak II 9+ Great slab climb! Start as in the preceding route, but traverse right 10 feet and climb the slab up the middle of the face following a line of 3 bolts--the first 2 straight up and the 3rd on the left. Mount a little pedestal above the 3rd bolt and make an exciting crux move to a jug before joining *Walt's Wall Route* on the ramp. (a.k.a. *Water Streak,* but a climb with that name was listed in a Vedauwoo guidebook many years prior to this route being climbed.)

15. Kopischka Finish 10a At the 3rd bolt of the preceding climb, traverse right to a 4th bolt before joining *Walt's Wall Route.*

16. Satterfield's Crack 8 and 16a Bolder Exit 9 This dramatic looking two pitch route ascends the huge dihedral corner formed between Walt's Wall and the Coke Bottle. Pitch 1 ascends the wide crack until a convenient belay can be made on a large boulder at the base of the upper part of the dihedral. The next pitch jams or liebacks the big corner until 10 feet before the top. At this point, enter a chimney on the right to end up on the ledge near the belay for last pitch of *Walt's Wall Route. The Bolder Exit* avoids the chimney by traversing left underneath a hanging boulder and then climbing up its left side, while the beginners on *Walt's Wall Route* look on with admiring glances.

Figure 3.3 Craig Luebben sans rope and rack on Horn's Mother (11a).

COKE BOTTLE

The huge bulging Coke Bottle (Figs. 3.4-3.8) with steep walls on 3 sides has a wide variety of challenging routes. The left wall faces 230°, the center wall 140°, and the right side 70°. Unless otherwise indicated descent from these climbs is most easily done by rappelling from the top of *Fourth of July Crack* (two ropes or one rope and some 3rd class scrambling). The next 2 climbs are area classics.

17. Fourth of July Crack 12a This challenging and sustained route is the left-most crack on the left wall. Start from the end of Pitch 1 of *Satterfield's Crack*. Stem and finger jam your way up to the relatively moderate offwidth exit. Lots of small gear (a.k.a. *Hard Promises*).

18. Horn's Mother 11a After 10 feet of rattly fists you'll feel like Whistler's Mother. One of those "it's there climbs." If you don't do it, you'll need an excuse as to why not. This is the right crack on the wall. Climb the overhanging fist jam (crux) to a small cave and belay. The 2nd pitch goes up the slanting, sustained 5.10 crack which can take a good many #3 and #4 Friends.

19. Silver Salute 13b A modern marvel. It is seldom climbed despite its magnificent position and good protection. Start from the right end of the belay ledge for *Walt's Wall Route* (or be a hard man/woman and start by climbing the crux of *Horn's Mother*). Then traverse horizontally following the line of bolts around the corner (crux). Continue until meeting up with *Light From Blue Horses*.

A girdle is a traverse encircling a crag and much in vogue in England. The next route is Vedauwoo's closest approach to this type of British favorite.

20. The 12th of Never 10c Ladies, girdles are back in fashion. Make your boyfriend go second, and scare the hell out of him. Begin with the 5.8 offwidth start of *Bell Crack,* and then traverse left along the horizontal crack above the base of the Bottle's projection going all the way to the left end of the Bottle. The crux is the final 10 feet just before stemming across a gap. Some big pieces, #4 Camalot and up, are required to protect this section. Belay just past the gap on a comfortable ledge. Descend by walking off to the left. The route would probably be harder going left to right (originally an aid line known as *Frontal Traverse*).

21. Boardwalk 11b Classic. Same start as *Bell Crack* but at the shelf traverse left and set up a semi-hanging belay below the obvious finger/hand crack. The second pitch ascends the flaring crack with the crux in the first 20 feet.

22. Light From Blue Horses 11c Start on the preceding climb. Just past its crux, traverse left following bolts to a hanging belay. Gallop through a line of bolts and bulges to a commodious shelf. This is a splendid finish for the preceding climb.

THE COKE BOTTLE
Left Wall

16. Satterfield's Crack 8
17. Fourth of July Crack 12a
18. Horn's Mother 11a
19. Silver Salute 13b

Figure 3.4

Figure 3.5 Todd Skinner on the first ascent of *Silver Salute* (13b). Despite it's magnificent position, it is seldom repeated. Wonder why? Photograph Courtesy of Piana/Cowboyography

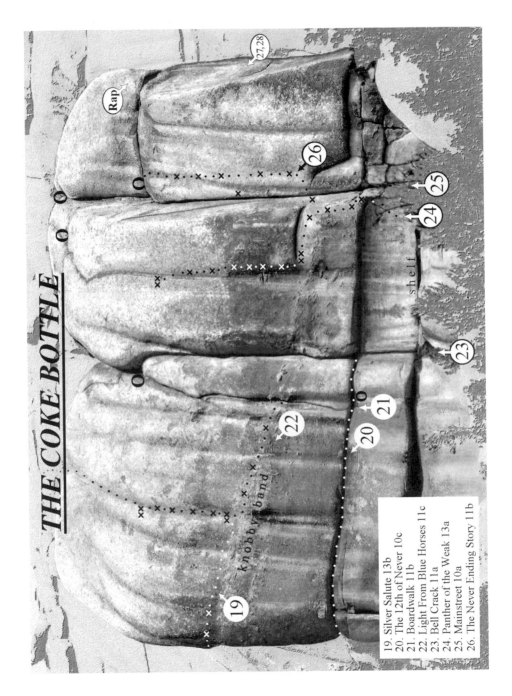

THE COKE BOTTLE

Rap

27,28

26

25
24
23
22
21
20
19

shelf

knobby band

19. Silver Salute 13b
20. The 12th of Never 10c
21. Boardwalk 11b
22. Light From Blue Horses 11c
23. Bell Crack 11a
24. Panther of the Weak 13a
25. Mainstreet 10a
26. The Never Ending Story 11b

Figure 3.6

23. Bell Crack 11a The obvious bell shaped crack towards the right side of the wall. If you can get into it, you've got it.

24. Panther of the Weak 13a Two bolts leading left can be seen low on the left face of the Mainstreet dihedral (sticking clipping the first bolt seems prudent). Climb the thin crack below the bolts, and then follow the bolts to the front face of the Coke Bottle to a rappel station below a large horizontal slot. This route is a charming diversion from the serious cracks located in this section of the Coke Bottle. The line of bolts above the belay station is, as of this writing, part of an uncompleted project.

25. Mainstreet 10a Awe the tourons in the parking lot as you strut downtown. The climb starts in the offwidth formed between the main bulge and the smaller bulge to the right. The crux is the first 20 feet. The upper section, which has 2 bolts, is mostly sustained 5.8-9 offwidth. A medium stopper can be used at the beginning and then nothing smaller than a #2 Big Bro. After 125 feet, belay between blocks in a little alcove (only slings needed). Climb the 5.8 V-slot on the left, or take the easier exit straight ahead.

26. The Never Ending Story 11b Traverse right from the lower bolt on the upper section of *Mainstreet*, follow a line of bolts up some very thin slab climbing to a small ledge, and then traverse left to join the *Mainstreet* belay. Finish on a *Mainstreet* exit. Combined with the start of *Mainstreet* this provides 120 feet of spectacular climbing from offwidth to thin slab and is a tribute to the skill and imagination of Layne Kopischka.

The next 2 routes are located on the northeast facing wall at the very right end of the Coke Bottle. They are bolt protected climbs sporting their way up the steep, imposing face--virtually vertical slab climbing. Descent is from rappel bolts (2 ropes) or Walt's Wall walkoff.

27. Space Oddity 12a A new classic. How steep can a slab climb get? Clamber up the chimney beneath the route, step right, and follow the bolts to the top. There are no moves harder than 5.11 and no moves easier than 5.11. (a.k.a. *Significant Locals*)

28. Young Guns 13a This version is a vast improvement over the TV program. Same start as *Space Oddity*, but follow the right line of bolts with an obvious crux at the 6 inch overhang above the 5th bolt. Only straight shooters will hit the target on this extremely sustained line.

29. TM Chimney 7+ A very classy chimney. Two pitches are inside the rock all the way, yet second pitch has exposure. It can be approached either from the left side of the Clam Shell or from the left side of the huge boulder left of the Clam

Figure 3.7 Liz Grenard strutting up *Mainstreet* (10a) -- a classic wide, plumb line. Photograph courtesy of Craig Luebben

Shell. Transcendental meditation needed to squeeze past the crux. Start at the right end of the Bottle under the page formed by the outer wall, and continue straight up gradually veering right to the light. Then traverse left back into the chimney working past a large chockstone, and belay on the obvious ledge. Pitch 2 goes left to a small right facing wall. Continue chimneying until you can escape left (continuing straight up is unprotected). A moderate but well spaced rack is needed for this climb. Traditional rating for this climb is 5.6 (a.k.a. *Thomas-Magary Chimney* and *Thomas-McGary Chimney*. McGary is probably the correct spelling).

FALL WALL AREA

This is the area of low angle slabs to the right of the Coke Bottle. It contains enticing slab routes, has the morning sun, is easily accessible, and thus sees a lot of traffic. There is a horizontal ledge/overhang running along the middle of the wall. The area above this is Upper Fall Wall and below Lower Fall Wall (Figs. 3.8-3.9) The right end of the wall lying below the overhang is the Cold Finger Area. There are rappel bolts at the top of *Fallout* (2 ropes), *Fall Wall Route, 5.11 Crack,* and *Micky Mantle.* You can also descend from Upper Fall Wall by scrambling northwest and hooking up with the Walt's Wall descent. There are rappel descents from either end of the Cold Finger Area.

30. Fallout 9 Start at *TM Chimney,* but as soon as feasible go right onto the wall near a flake. Then climb up the outside of the page formed between the Coke Bottle and Lower Fall Wall. (A direct start to the right is harder and does not protect.) Combination of face climbing and offwidth. There is one bolt en route. Belay at the start of *Micky Mantle.* Choose a second pitch from Upper Fall Wall (*Neon Madman* recommended), or rappel off.

31. Neon Madman 10a This is the thin crack at the left end of Upper Fall Wall. Fun climbing in an exposed position. No move is harder than 9+, and protection is adequate but requires skill to set--take many small pieces (a.k.a. *Neon Cowboy*).

32. Micky Mantle 10c Two yards to the right of *Neon Madman* is a nice slab route that follows 4 bolts to the top. You can protect getting to the first bolt by placing a stopper on a long sling in *Neon Madman.*

33. Krypton Sociopath 11a A toprope problem that ascends the trough 2 yards right of *Micky Mantle.*

34. Argon Depressive 11a A toprope problem that ascends the second trough right of *Micky Mantle.*

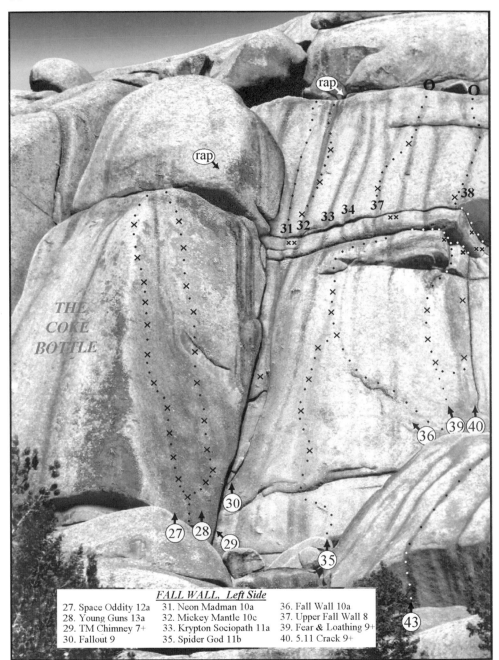

Figure 3.8

FALL WALL, Left Side

27. Space Oddity 12a	31. Neon Madman 10a	36. Fall Wall 10a
28. Young Guns 13a	32. Mickey Mantle 10c	37. Upper Fall Wall 8
29. TM Chimney 7+	33. Krypton Sociopath 11a	39. Fear & Loathing 9+
30. Fallout 9	35. Spider God 11b	40. 5.11 Crack 9+

The Hole

O

38

41

45

48

40 42 44 46

47

The Clamshell Boulder

FALL WALL, Right Side

40. 5.11 Crack 9+   45. Easy Overhang Traverse 8
41. Colonial Rule 11a   46. E.O. Friction 5
42. Gunga Din 11a   47. Cold Fingers 7
44. E.O. Lieback 5   48. Hole 7

Figure 3.9

35. Spider God 11b This is a demanding, alternate start to *Fall Wall Route*. Twelve yards to the right of *TM Chimney* is a large slanting boulder at the end of the grassy shelf. Scramble onto it for the belay. Stretch over to the main wall using a small diagonal rib and aim towards the first bolt. A small camming unit can be set in the horizontal crack below the bolt. Then follow the line of 5 bolts which first go a little left before going right. After the last bolt, head for the 2nd bolt on *Fall Wall Route*.

36. Fall Wall Route 10a Super classic. Belay 3 yards left of *5.11 Crack*. Make a rising traverse left for 30 feet to a flake of questionable integrity where a #3 Friend can be placed (7). The exposure is immediate and a fall unthinkable. Continue the traverse to the first bolt, and climb straight up to the next 2 bolts. Traverse left a few feet and move up (crux) to the crack (#1.5 or #2 Friend) at the base of the headwall. Traverse right two feet and surmount the headwall. Experience indicates this last move is best done promptly.

36a. Last of the Elfin Boltmen 11a The climbing is fine, but the protection is next to nonexistent. Climb to the flake on *Fall Wall Route*. Now climb up to the tiny right facing dihedral below the overhang. It is midway between the exits on *Fall Wall Route* and *Fear and Loathing*. Move left an arm's length, and struggle up using a black knob.

37. Upper Fall Wall Route 8 From the belay on *Fall Wall Route* climb straight up to a bolt. Go slightly right towards a second bolt, and climb to a very small shelf which takes very small gear. Finish up the runout face. Belay from bolts atop *Micky Mantle*. (The first ascent party used an easier but more runout start. They started climbing 10 feet right of the belay, went straight up, and headed back left.)

38. Middle Road 10a You can get to the start of this route in 2 different ways. Start as for the preceding route but traverse right until in the trough above *Colonial Rule*. The trough contains one bolt about 10 feet up and is runout and flaky. The most obvious way to get to the route is to climb *Colonial Rule* for which this trough is the natural finish (*Middle Road* was first climbed by P. Koedt and J. Mathiessen in December 1965 with only a bolt at the start and rated 5.8. Agh!)

39. Fear and Loathing 9+ Climb to the first bolt on *5.11 Crack,* traverse left (crux), climb past 3 bolts to a little headwall on the right with a right facing dihedral corner. Hand jam the dihedral crack and traverse left to the top of *Fall Wall Route*. Variations: for a more natural but unprotected start climb straight up to the first bolt (9); for a more unnatural exit traverse right after the last bolt to the top of *5.11 Crack*. Double ropes reduce drag, especially for the last variation.

40. 5.11 Crack 9+ Climb the crack (2 bolts) to the rappel station under the roof. Bring lots of small gear: the crux is clipping the first bolt which is a long way off the deck; the 2nd bolt is 15 feet from the first bolt. A really fun climb with interesting moves and protection .

41. Colonial Rule 11a From atop *5.11 Crack* climb out the roof to a little shelf on the left and continue up *Middle Road.* An unappealing alternate to *Middle Road,* and chosen by many, is to just downclimb to the Fall Wall Ledge. Upon completing the first ascent of this route in 1897, Rudyard Kipling exclaimed, "You're a better man than I am..."

42. Gunga Din 11a Just right of *5.11 Crack* is a short left facing dihedral above which are 3 bolts. Small gear protects getting to the first bolt past which are the crux moves to the 2nd bolt. From there move up a few feet, go right to the 3rd bolt, and bear left heading to the belay station.

43. Clam Shell 5 Leaning against Fall Wall is a huge clam shell shaped rock. Jump on to it (literally) and climb to the top. A toprope problem without protection.

44. E.O. Lieback 5 A little right of *Gunga Din* is right facing, low angle dihedral. Climb this to the roof where there are rappel bolts. Options: rappel or climb the next route (a.k.a. *Easy Lieback*).

45. Easy Overhang Traverse 8 From the top of the preceding route make a tricky 5.8 move left onto the face and traverse left (6) all the way to the top of *Fall Wall Route.*

46. E.O.Friction 5 Nice way to learn slab climbing. A yard right of *E.O. Lieback* is a line of bolts. Go left at the last bolt aiming for the top of *E.O. Lieback.* (a.k.a. *Easy Friction*)

47. Cold Finger 7 Classic moderate slab. After graduating from the preceding route, move 3 yards right to a line of 4 bolts leading to an I-bolt where the following options are available : (i) rappel; (ii) traverse left to *Easy Overhang Traverse*; (iii) finish with *Hole* (highly recommended). (a.k.a *Cold Fingers*)

48. Hole 7 Excellent position and exposure. Traverse right from the preceding belay, jam a short, easy crack, squiggle up an easy 10 foot chimney formed by a flake and the left wall, and belay at the base of a slabby bulge. Climb the bulge (7) and enter the obvious hole. Climb out its left side (crux--protects with large piece) and then up the left facing dihedral. Continue for ten feet to a belay off a tree.

Fifty yards south of the Clam Shell is a another huge boulder with 2 routes on it.

49. Whistling Jupiter 12b Follow the bolts up the west face of the boulder entering a shallow groove after the precipitous start.

50. Veda-Voodoo 12a Follow the bolts up the north face.

MASTER BLASTER AREA

This area is to the left of Walt's Wall Area and to the left and well below Hassler's Hatbox (Fig. 3.10). There are two distinct approaches dictated, in part, by what you intend to climb. Both approaches will allow you to access climbs in either the lower or upper section. However, the first approach is most efficient for climbs in the lower part (i.e., from *Blaster Junior* to *Trip Master*) while the second approach is best for the upper part (i.e., from *Homecoming* to *Drip Drop*).

The first approach takes the Turtle Rock Trail towards Holy Saturday. Two prominent gullies go uphill (right) after you emerge from the aspen grove. Scramble up either one for approximately 200 yards. You will reach a 50 foot high headwall split in half by a horizontal fissure. The headwall lies underneath a huge boulder. This headwall is at the lower end of the Master Blaster Area and is the site of *Blaster Junior*. The second approach will be discussed below.

51. Blaster Junior 10a Climb the right side of a partially detached flake to the large horizontal crack. Step left and continue up a bulging hand crack. Belay beneath the huge boulder. Take extra Friends in the range #2.5-#4.

The start of *Dirty Pictures* is about 20 yards to the right of the belay for *Blaster Junior*. Alternately, scramble right around the base of the headwall for about 12 yards, and 3rd class up the first wide crack on the left to get to the start. (The approach from the top of the Walt's Wall Area is more complicated but is mentioned here for completeness. Scramble down the left side of the down sloping wall mentioned below, continue on for another 50 yards, turn right, and scramble through the boulders before heading northeast for another 33 yards.)

52. Dirty Pictures From The Prom 8+ Pictures from the prom fell out of a backpack and became soiled. At the start surmount a 6 foot wall at either of two cracks, and traverse right along a low angle slab until a face with 2 bolts can be seen. At (but not above) the 2nd bolt traverse right a short distance and then up into a right facing dihedral which forms an offwidth at its top. The climbing is sustained and varied.

For the next climb, continue approximately 75 yards up the gully to the right of the *Blaster Junior* headwall. Go into an area strewn with large, piled up boulders forming caves and drop-offs.

53. Trip Master Monkey 12b Up and to your left just before entering the first large cave is a very overhung, wide crack about 30 feet off the deck. What follows is super classic Leavittation-- you feet will be above your head most of the way--if you still have your head on after trying to climb this.

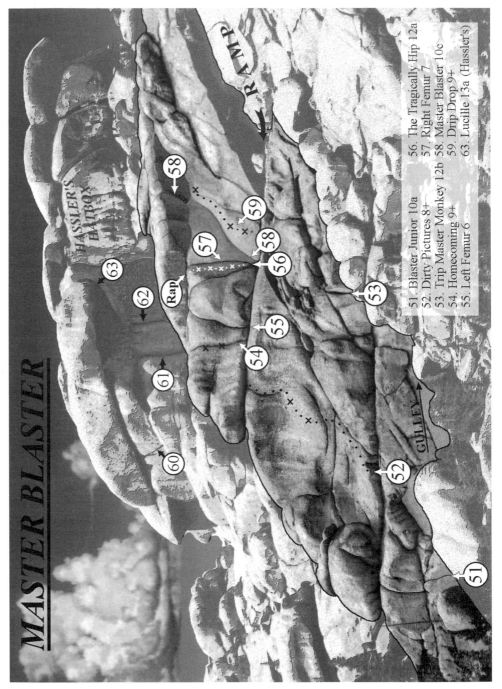

MASTER BLASTER

HASSLER'S BAITBOX

RAMP

GULLEY

Rap

51. Blaster Junior 10a
52. Dirty Pictures 8+
53. Trip Master Monkey 12b
54. Homecoming 9+
55. Left Femur 6

56. The Tragically Hip 12a
57. Right Femur 7
58. Master Blaster 10c
59. Drip Drop 9+
63. Lucille 13a (Hassler's)

Figure 2.10

Figure 3.11 Bob Scarpelli casually climbing with his feet above his head on his route, *Trip Master Monkey* (12b). Photo courtesy of Craig Luebben.

The second approach to Master Blaster area starts by climbing any route on the Walt's Wall Area. Continue straight on for 33 yards from the top of *Edwards' Crack*. Turn left for 25 yards until you come to the edge of a downward sloping wall facing 230°. The overhanging *Master Blaster* crack can be seen to the right on a wall oriented at 140°. Scramble down either the left or right end of the sloping wall to get to the base of the upper section climbs. They are located along the shelf on which *Dirty Pictures* ends and on which *Master Blaster* begins. Once on the shelf traverse left (west) along the shelf. The first of these climbs, which is the farthest left, begins just right of the exit to *Dirty Pictures*.

54. Homecoming 9+ This nice little climb is a serious lead despite the two bolts. Ascend a shallow trough past the two bolts.

55. Left Femur 6 Climb the wide crack formed by the big flake and the back wall a little to the left of the next climb.

56. The Tragically Hip 12a A very demanding climb up a face and thin seam with friable rock. This formerly dangerous climb now has enough bolts to make it less tragic but not secure.

57. Right Femur 7 Climb the wide crack just right of *The Tragically Hip*.

58. Master Blaster 10c Test piece. Climb the right facing dihedral (10a), and set a belay below the overhanging hand/fist crack. Power up it. Gear consists of (at least) #1-#4 Camalots with small and medium stoppers.

59. Drip Drop 9+ A nice alternate first pitch to *Master Blaster*--harder than it looks. The line follows the two bolts up the face to the right of *Master Blaster* and joins *Blaster* at the start of its 2nd pitch.

Hassler's Hatbox

As you enter the Central Area, Hassler's Hatbox, a large blocky structure with distinct vertical walls and with an overhanging roof at either end, can easily be seen sitting high atop the Walt's Wall Area (Figs. 3.12-3.13). The usual approach to the Hatbox consists in climbing a route on Walt's Wall and continuing straight on for about 150 yards. Alternately, you can hike in by going uphill and sharply left (southwest) at the end of Robbers' Roost Road from where you can see the finish to *Journey to Coramonde*. There are rappel bolts atop *Cat's Cradle* and *The Tragically Hip*. Also, you can downclimb from the top of the Hatbox by continuing to the north and then turning northeast following any of several gullies to the end of Robbers' Roost Road. The routes on the left side of the Hatbox start on a shelf about 15 feet below the routes on the right. An exception to this description is the outlying *Strained Tendons* for which the approach and descent are unique.

60. Strained Tendons 9+ Good climb for alpine training--it'll take you all day to get there. Hike towards Holy Saturday along the Turtle Rock Trail. About half way there find a gully on the right facing southwest. At the top of the gully and to the left of *Lucille* is a left slanting handcrack on a wall facing southwest. Hike up the gully which is easier said than done. Climb the handcrack and descend from slings around a chockstone.

61. Victory of Defeat 10b Winning or losing, this route provides fine, varied climbing from face to offwidth and lots in between. The crux is getting past the big knob on the right near the start. The traverse to *Lucille* is disappointingly easy.

62. Best of the Blues 10b The only reason to climb this stupid route is to get to *Lucille*. It's a walk up to the overhanging crack and then one hard move.

63. Lucille 13a This big overhanging offwidth is on the right side of the roof at the left side of Hassler's Hatbox. If you need advice, don't bother climbing this route. This spectacular crack, which is a world class standard for offwidth, has yet to see a second ascent.

64. Hassler's Hatbox Route 7- Innovative and classic. A little to the right of the *Lucille* roof is a dihedral corner that, 25 feet up, has a tunnel like appearance. Climb this to the top and finish with the short crawl off exit to the right. Mostly 6 (traditional rating) with two isolated moves of 7.

65. Hassler's Right 9 Start 7 yards to the right of the preceding route in a crack that begins as an offwidth (9), turns into stemming before presenting an overhanging wide crack. Helpful chockstones are found along the way.

44

Figure 3.12 *Lucille* (13a) is the awesome, overhanging crack. Good test piece for those aspiring to lead 5.13.

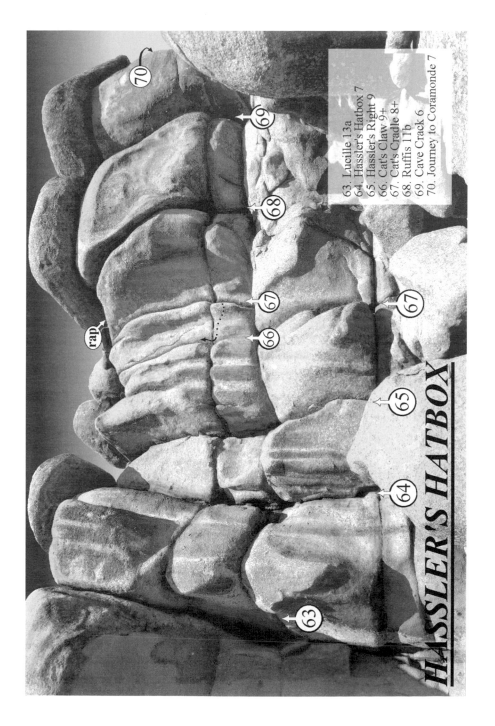

63. Lucille 13a
64. Hassler's Hatbox 7
65. Hassler's Right 9
66. Cat's Claw 9+
67. Cat's Cradle 8+
68. Ruffis 11b
69. Cave Crack 6
70. Journey to Coramonde 7

HASSLER'S HATBOX

Figure 3.13

66. Cat's Claw 9+ Same start as 2nd pitch of *Cat's Cradle*. Place protection in *Cat's Cradle*, and traverse left around the bulge (crux, TCU) into a 5.8 hand crack.

67. Cat's Cradle 8+ The reference is to Vonnegut and not literal. Seven yards right of *Hassler's Right* is an opening with a V shaped slot. Climb out the right side of the slot to a ledge, traverse right 5 feet to the rightmost crack on this section formed by a rib and the face on the right (oriented at 220°). Belay. The start of the second pitch is a 5.9 boulder problem after which splendid hand jamming and not pussy footing will get you to the top. The first pitch can be avoided (not recommended) by approaching the 2nd pitch from the right

68. Ruffis 11b Classic. An overhanging, finger crack start (crux) is followed by a deceptively strenuous hand crack (a.k.a. *Roofus*).

69. Cave Crack 6 Spelunkers' delight. Climb the chockstone and look around for the secret crack. RP's to #3 Friend. A big piece is needed for the belay. For descent scramble to the top of *Cat's Cradle*.

70. Journey To Coramonde 7 Chimney past a big boulder on the right end of the shelf to get to the platform beneath the huge roof dominating the right end of Hassler's Hatbox. The climb starts in a right facing dihedral crack. Climb it to the roof, and do an airy traverse right. Continue around a corner until a gear belay can be set up. Same descent as for *Cave Crack*.

Figure 3.14 Rob Kelman getting cloned on Cat's Cradle (8+).

HOLY SATURDAY

"And on the seventh day God rested." After taking the Vedauwoo turnoff, the prominent overhanging wall of *Holy Saturday* (cleft in two by *Hide-A-Way Chimney)* appears on the left (west) at 0.8 mile along the road. This peaceful, close-in spot does not get much traffic and is the perfect setting for Sabbath climbing. To get there, continue for 0.6 mile after making the turn towards the central area, turn left (south) and go to the parking area at the road's end. The Turtle Rock Trail heads west from there. Walk along it for about three eighths of a mile at which point the unmistakable south by southeast facing wall of Holy Saturday comes into view (Figs. 3.15-3.16). Descent is by rappel bolts to the right of *Hide-A-Way Chimney* or walkoff on the northwest side. *Hume-Annoyed* faces 230°, the main wall faces 160°, and the wall around the corner to the right is at 60°.

71. Hume-Annoyed From Dixie 11c Just around the corner left of *Route of All Evil,* a crack in an open book reaches to a roof and jogs left 2 feet as it bypasses the roof. Follow the crack using humanoid ingenuity to set adequate but not comforting protection.

72. Route of All Evil 11a This sustained climb starts near the left end of the wall beneath an offwidth situated 10 feet above the deck. Climb through the offwidth (crux) to a platform below two cracks forming a V. Ascend the right leaning crack.

Fifteen yards from the left edge of the wall two parallel cracks can be seen-- *Passover* on the left and *Zealot* on the right. These are demanding climbs that only a zealot would try because poorly set protection could result in becoming a sacrificial lamb.

73. Passover 11b Begin in a thin crack that enlarges to a hand crack after 10 feet. At the small roof traverse right (crux) passing over to *Zealot.*

74. Zealot 11b Start by bouldering hard face moves until you get to a skimpy crack. Continue up a slot to a window.

75. Hide-A-Way Chimney 5 Looks are deceiving--this classic climb is not 5.10 since there are lots of handholds hidden inside.

76. Flake 8+ One of the best pitches of 5.8 at Vedauwoo--offwidth to a titillating finish on the face, exposure all the way, and sustained. A widely spaced rack will keep you from flaking off. Start around the corner at the right end of the wall taking the left most crack. After 25 feet, traverse right into the next crack, moving onto the face when the crack ends.

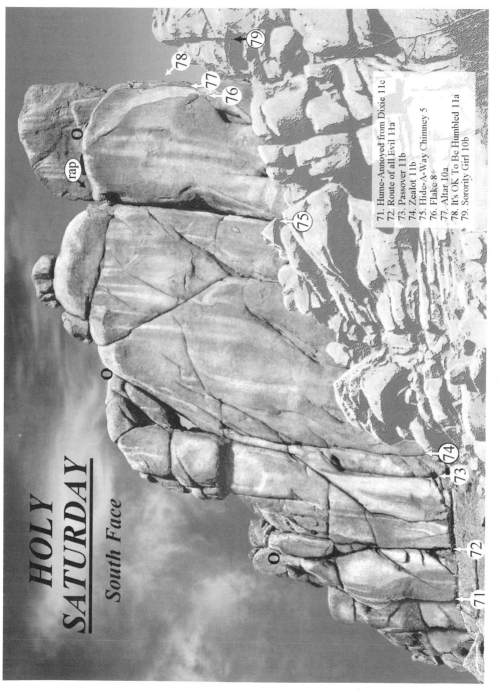

HOLY SATURDAY *South Face*

71. Hume-Annoyed from Dixie 11c
72. Route of all Evil 11a
73. Passover 11b
74. Zealot 11b
75. Hide-A-Way Chimney 5
76. Flake 8+
77. Altar 10a
78. It's OK To Be Humbled 11a
79. Sorority Girl 10b

Figure 3.15

Figure 3.16

77. Altar 10a Start about 3 yards right of *Flake* and climb a few feet of face to a wide crack. The crux is entering the crack--a move which was once 5.7 but, as flakes kept breaking off, became more difficult. Climbing is strenuous but gradually eases up. The second pitch of *It's OK To Be Humbled* serves as a nice, consistent finish for this route.

78. It's OK To Be Humbled 11a If you get past the crux in the middle of the first pitch, you might as well be proud. It's best done in two pitches with the first belay on the big ledge. The route starts in the crack two yards right of *Altar*. The second pitch, which is 10a, starts 10 feet to the right of the end of the first pitch. Rappel off a cable.

79. Sorority Girl 10b Move northeast across the gap at the northeast end of Holy Saturday. A prominent dihedral will be visible on your left. Its left wall faces south by southeast. Climb the crack in the dihedral.

FOREIGN TERRITORY

This area has just a few established climbs, but all are of high quality. Like Jurassic Park, it is often sheltered from the wind. Consequently, the routes on its north wall (which faces south) often provide pleasant climbing when more exposed areas are less inviting. Contrariwise, the north facing climbs here never see the sun. To get to Foreign Territory, walk about 50 yards past Holy Saturday and scramble right (east) into a gully the right side of which is formed by the north wall of Holy Saturday. The first three climbs are on the north side of the area (Fig. 3.17B).

80. Who The *Devil* is Charlie Creese? 10a This is a very short bottomless handcrack just left of *Wild Thing*. (The climb was originally given a less acceptable name by Paul Piana. Now that he is more mature, he agrees to the name change.)

81. Wild Thing 10b This crack starts in a left facing dihedral and evolves from hands to slightly offwidth as it proceeds through 3 small, but prominent, roofs. Two of the roofs are on the left, and the other is on the right.

82. Japan Club 10d This is a straight up crack climb that starts below the left side of prominent roof. It is directly across from *London Calling*.

The remaining climbs are on the south side of the area. They start in an obvious 25 foot high, arch shaped alcove (Fig. 3.17A).

83. London Calling 11d Start about 3 yards left of *Nasty Crack*, and follow the thin crack through the multiple roof structure.

84. Nasty Crack 12a Start in a left facing dihedral with a vertical right wall. Climb about three fourths the way up the dihedral, and then surmount the right wall and escape via a hand crack.

Figure 3.17

JURASSIC PARK

Jurassic Park (Fig. 3.18) has remained largely undeveloped, despite its location within the heart of Vedauwoo. In fact, no other climbers were encountered there throughout the '93 climbing season. Reasons for this are unclear, although the authors frequently heard sounds resembling the feeding calls of large animals. This phenomenon was caused, most probably, by wind howling through the dense stands of aspens and pine across the valley. Notwithstanding the unsettling nature of these sounds, the area has a southern, sunny exposure and is sheltered from the wind making it a pleasant place to climb, especially on windy days.

To get to Jurassic Park hike 220 yards past Holy Saturday where a 15 foot high pile of rocks is encountered on the right side of the trail. Just past the pile a faint trail strikes immediately uphill to the right, continues up and through Jurassic Pass and back down again into Jurassic Park proper. As the Park is entered, the 150 yard long climbing wall, which runs from west to east, is on the left. The routes begin on the west end behind the Juvenile Raptor Boulder.

Climbing consists of 18 rather short, yet challenging lines from 6 to 11, that offer a lot of technical variety and for which a half-rack usually suffices. A conveniently located rappel station is above *CC Left,* and another is 10 yards right of *Get Up That Tree.* There is a downclimb 30 yards to the right of *Epilogue.*

85. Prologue 6 Start in a chimney in back of the Juvenile Raptor. After 25 feet enter a hand crack which diagonals up and left for 35 feet. Take two #2.5 and #3.5 Friends.

86. Recombination Mutation 7 Begin in the preceding chimney. Combine and recombine hand jams all the way. An excellent route for learning hand jams, but tape or your hands will be mutated.

An alternate start (8) for the preceding routes uses the Sternal Groove at the front of the Juvenile Raptor.

87. First Iteration 10a Immediately right of the Juvenile Raptor, follow a line of 3 bolts and end on a shelf about 50 feet above. Finish on the exit crack of the next climb, or scramble up and left. Two horizontal cracks offer marginal protection using small gear.

88. Sore-O-Pod 8 Fifty feet of textbook 5.8 hand jams lead to a shelf and a short headwall with 5.7 hand jams. Extra #2.5 to #3.5 Friends.

JURASSIC PARK

SHELF · ROOF

SHELF

S H E L F

rap

rap

JR

85. Prologue 6
86. Recombination 7
87. First Iteration 10a
88. Sore-O-Pod 8
89. CC Left 9
90. Crichton's Crack 11c

91. Flake-O-Saurus 10c
92. Get Up That Tree 8
93. A Lawyer on the Toilet 8
94. Slot-A-Saurus 9+
95. Lichen Lung 10d
96. Mud in Your Eye 11b

97. Velociraptor's Revenge 11b A1
98. Triceratops I 10c
99. Triceratops II 10c
100. Triceratops III 10c
101. Digiripper Raptoris 10a
102. Epilogue 7 (not shown)

TO JURASSIC PASS

Figure 3.18

89. CC Left 9 Ascend the next route for about 40 feet, bear left, and mount large irregular flakes to the roof which is passed more easily than it looks from the ground.

90. Crichton's Crack 11c This route requires varied techniques: stemming and jamming (9), problematic bottomed out fingers (11b), and lastly off fist and off-width to get through the bulging crux roof.

91. Flake-O-Saurus 10c Jam up a right facing and overhanging 30 foot flake with some dicey face work after leaving the crack. Finish on any of the preceding routes, or scramble down to the right.

Descent for the remaining climbs is from the rappel station to the right of *Get Up That Tree* or by walkdown 30 yards right of *Epilog.*

92. Get Up That Tree 8 ... or the Procompsognathid may get you! Move past the two large chockstones and bypass an inverted skeletal tree having origins in a time long past.

93. A Lawyer On The Toilet 8 A surprise beginning (7 offwidth) and even more surprising (thin 8) when grunting for the finish.

94. Slot-A-Saurus 9+ Start in (or out of) the slot, and turn a corner for a crack going from fingers to hands (35 feet). The final roof is short and challenging. This is the longest route on the wall.

95. Lichen Lung 10d A Bob Scarpelli classic--sustained and bulging off fingers to hands. Don't breathe too deeply, or the lichen may become a permanent pulmonary passenger. Extra #1.5 to #2.5 Friends.

96. Mud In Your Eye 11b A harder version of the preceding climb. After the shelf is attained, finish on the headwall of *Lichen Lung,* or scramble to the top.

97. Velociraptor's Revenge 11b A1 Careful! This is a mean people eater. Use a bolt and aiders in the unprotected, overhanging and bottomed out slot at the beginning. A hand crack begins 25 feet off the deck, turns into fingers, and terminates in a devious exit onto a shelf. Continue up an obvious short line in the headwall (10a).

The next 3 climbs have different beginnings and endings, but en route all funnel through the same crux--a voracious, overhanging, offwidth crack (#3 Big Bro) that pierces the roof at the right end of a big block. This crack lies directly above *Tri-cera-tops II.* Beware of popcorn granite beneath the roof on the aptly named Coprolith Ledge. Above the roof are 3 short cracks (9) on a headwall. Each crack is a finish for one of the climbs.

98. Tri-cera-tops I 10c Climb a right facing dihedral (8) to Coprolith Ledge, traverse right, and surmount the crux crack. Finish on the left exit crack.

99. Tri-cera-tops II 10c Climb a left leaning crack which requires steep liebacking (9) and leads to an obvious Pterodactyl aerie. Traverse right on Coprolith Ledge to the crux crack, and finish on the middle exit crack.

100. Tri-cera-tops III 10c Climb a right leaning, bulgy hand and finger crack (10b) that peters out and turns into dicey, exposed face. At Coprolith Ledge traverse left to the crux crack, and take the right exit crack.

101. Digiripper Raptoris 10a Reputed to eat flesh in the finger slots. Once past this digital threat, jog slightly right on Coprolith Ledge, and take the chimney exit of *Epilog*.

102. Epilog 7 Take a left, upward slanting groove (15 yards right of *Digiripper*) to a chimney exit. A vertical crack line on the back wall of the chimney accepts protection for this typical Vedauwoo struggle.

4. NORTHEAST CENTRAL

Northeast Central is a sprawling massif that completes the huge horseshoe shaped structure forming the Central Area (see Fig. 1.4). It affords many opportunities for less crowded climbing than Southwest Central, but it is still readily accessible. The routes will be described starting at the end of Robbers' Roost Road moving counterclockwise (east) from the westerly end. The sprawling, disjointed nature of this formation should be emphasized, since a mistake on the approach will belie the assertion of accessibility.

GLEN DOME

Glen Dome is the first major prominence on the right as you look west from the end of the road. The following routes are approached by hiking west up the old nature trail almost until the crest is reached and then traversing right. These routes are on a wall facing 150°. Descent is a walkdown to the northeast.

1. Glenn's First Name 4 There is a low angled hand crack twelve yards to the right of the trail. It arches upward for 100 feet of good jam practice.

2. Water Streak 7 As you look west from the end of the road, two water streaks can be seen (sometimes obscured in the late afternoon by the glancing sun) to the right of *Route 1*. Belay 2 yards to the right of the streaks on a comfortable platform. Climb the face between the streaks into a left facing dihedral, and follow it to the top (130 feet). There is no protection on the face between the streaks, making the first part (crux) of the climb a risky proposition.

TURTLE ROCK

Just after entering the Vedauwoo turnoff, the striking *Straight and Narrow* dihedral can be seen on Turtle Rock--due east and high atop the left end of Northeast Central. There are two major climbing areas on Turtle Rock--Heartbreak Hotel and Land of the Rising Moon. *Straight and Narrow* is in the middle of the Land of the Rising Moon, while Heartbreak Hotel is around the far side of the rock. Most of the routes in the Hotel face north.

HEARTBREAK HOTEL

Here's how to get to Heartbreak Hotel. Take the path to Crystal Freeway as far as the low point of the saddle between Turtle Rock and Friction Tower. Then go left (northwest) up the southeast facing slabs following a line of pine trees until reaching the upper walls of Turtle Rock. Then go right (counterclockwise) for

Figure 4.1 The crux move on Beta Blocker (5.8).

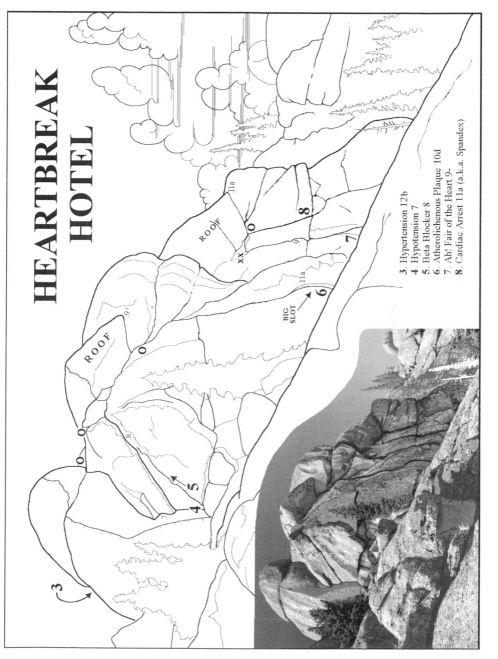

HEARTBREAK HOTEL

3. Hypertension 12b
4. Hypotension 7
5. Beta Blocker 8
6. Atherolichenous Plaque 10d
7. Ah! Fair of the Heart 9-
8. Cardiac Arrest 11a (a.k.a. Spandex)

Figure 4.2

about 65 yards (Fig. 4.2). Sometimes odd things happen up here. There have been sightings of an older man with turned up collar and spangles soloing the routes while singing old rock songs.

3.   Hypertension 12b A 40 foot finger crack (crux) sits in front of a pile of boulders. The crack starts in a right facing dihedral and points straight southeast. After this unintermittedly difficult beginning, follow the crack to an 11 roof and the top of the mound. Descent: continue past the belay, scramble up a friction face to the top of a mound, and walk left (southwest) until back on the lower slope beneath the climb. The name refers not to a condition of circulatory pathology but to the state of the rope holding those aspiring to be 5.12 leaders.

4.   Hypotension 7 Walk 50 yards or so around to the right (counterclockwise) from *Hypertension* to a wall facing 130°. Climb the crack in a dihedral corner that slants left then right, and finishes with a straight up exit. Mostly 5 with spots of 7. Descend as for *Hypertension.*

5.   Beta Blocker 8 There is a right leaning ramp and crack just past the start of *Hypotension*. Climb them to the end of the wall. Here's the Beta so you don't get blocked: set a #2.5 Friend before turning the corner (crux). Then climb a crack and a face to the top. Belay using a chockstone. Except for the amusing crux move, the climbing is easy.

The ratings on the next two routes reflect the current condition of the rock. If they get done more often, the ratings may get easier.

6.   Atherolichenous Plaque 10d Walk right from *Beta Blocker* around a corner to a wall facing 320°. The climb begins in 12 foot high offwidth slot (10d) which is 12 yards from the left end of the wall. Continue on a finger/hand crack and belay beneath a big roof. Pitch 2 passes the roof on the right (9+ and #4 Friend) and finishes in a 5.8 hand crack.

7.   Ah! Fair of the Heart 9- Thirteen yards right of the preceding climb is a slot leading to a bottomed out crack in a huge roof. Climb the crack to the rappel station at the base of the roof. Smooth, sustained climbing mostly at the 8 level. After completing the first ascent in 1962, Elvis Presley said, "Don't be cruel when you're at Heartbreak Hotel !"

8.   Spandex 11a Climb the crack of the preceding route for 20 feet and then traverse right on a ledge to a left facing dihedral. Climb the dihedral to the roof and belay (9). Pass the roof on the right (crux--#2 Lowe Ball) and belay about 15 feet higher. A short 8 pitch ends the climb. (a.k.a. *Cardiac Arrest*--a name more consistent with others on this cliff.)

Figure 4.3 Tim Williams alleviating his patient's *Cardiac Arrest (11a).*

LAND OF THE RISING MOON

To get to the next group of climbs, start up the old nature trail at the end of the parking lot. About half way up, past the No. 4 trail marker but before the wooden stairs, turn right up a faint trail. After 35 yards, head up left (west) and walk through a small grove. Then scramble up to the tower, gradually working right (north). The vertical crack of *Straight and Narrow* will soon come into view. To get to *Blade Runner* continue traversing left for another hundred yards or so until the distinctive wide crack of *Colorado Cable Cutter* becomes visible on a wall facing 220°.

9.   Colorado Cable Cutter 9+ Climb a 30 foot high offwidth that is 3 yards left of *Blade Runner.* Traverse left on easy ground to a right facing dihedral and climb it. Traverse left again to the next right facing dihedral and climb to the wide crack on the left. Ascend it to the top. This route is best done in 2 or 3 pitches to minimize rope drag. Descent: rappel to the left.

10. Blade Runner 11b Climb the thin crack in the right facing dihedral corner (right wall faces 330°). Protection is sparse on this Eldorado like dihedral-- otherwise, a very nice climb.

The two *Moon* climbs are on an overhanging wall (facing 260°) in which there is a right leaning offwidth with a chockstone in its middle. About 50 feet up, there is a short shelf going right . Downclimb a gully to the left to descend from these two recommended climbs. See Fig. 4.4.

11. Moonrise Variation 10d Ascend the right leaning offwidth until the narrow sloping shelf. Then follow an ever narrowing left leaning crack until the final face moves which can be done straight up or veering to the left. The crux is at the transition from the crack to face (medium stopper and a #1.5 Friend).

12. Moon Tide 10a Climb the preceding route to the down sloping shelf. Then traverse right along the shelf (crux) to the 12 foot offwidth, exit crack.

There is a south facing wall around the corner and to the right of *Straight and Narrow.* There is a low angle slab in front of the wall. The next 4 climbs are in this area. In particular, the next two climbs start in a short vertical crack 5 yards left of *Straight and Narrow* on a wall facing southeast. Both climbs are true test pieces.

13. Cross of Iron 12c Climb the vertical crack and move up left to an extremely thin vertical seam. Make a desperate iron cross move to a crack on the left. According to Scott Blunk, this climb protects OK. Let the reader beware.

Land of the
RISING MOON

9. Colo. Cable Cutter 9+
10. Blade Runner 11b
11. Moonrise Variation 10d
12. Moon Tide 10a
13. Cross of Iron 12c
14. Master of Sport 12b
15. Straight & Narrow 8+
16. Drain Pipe 6

Figure 4.4

Figure 4.5 A *Master of Sport* (12b), Paul Piana, on the first ascent of this route. Courtesy of Piana/Cowboyography

14. Master of Sport 12b After climbing the vertical crack, follow a right slanting crack containing one piton until you can (thankfully) stem over to *Straight and Narrow*. Be prepared to place protection from less than restful stances.

15. Straight and Narrow 8+ Classic. It looks like an offwidth and it feels like an offwidth, but it's not an offwidth. It's hand jamming and liebacking all the way along this superb route due to a double and triple crack system inside the big crack. Descent: involved walk off to the right, or rappel slings around a chock stone on the right. Alternately, continue up the crack for another pitch (3rd pitch of the next route).

16. Drain Pipe 4 Seventeen yards uphill from *Straight and Narrow* is a chimney that starts on the right side of a triangular block. Climb the chimney to just above the block. Then traverse left into another chimney, climb to a shelf and belay. Make an easy traverse left to the main wall and belay . Climb to the top via the wide crack in the dihedral corner. Descend by scrambling down the backside.

FRICTION TOWER

CRYSTAL FREEWAY

Friction Tower, the prominence to the right of Turtle Rock, lies directly northeast when viewed from the end of Robbers' Roost Road. Crystal Freeway (Fig. 4.6) is the wall on its northwest side (more precisely, the orientation is 340°) . It is the only developed area on Friction Tower. The most obvious approach to Crystal Freeway consists of hiking straight up the gully to the low point of the saddle between Turtle Rock and Friction Tower and looking for Crystal Freeway which will be on your right. An easier approach starts at the end of Robbers' Roost Road. Head uphill (north) for 50 yards and then slant to the right (east) and follow a line of three dead trees heading for the right (southwest) end of Crystal Freeway. Orienting routes on the wall are *Northeast Cutoff, Flake Out,* and *Strawberry Jam.*

The usual descent is from the rappel bolts at the top of *Exit Ramp* (two ropes!). Alternately, it can be done as two single ropes rappels utilizing a pair of intermediate rappel bolts (the second rappel is 82 feet!). There is also a walkdown. At the left end of the wall, downclimb to a little sloping shelf, jump to a flat area and downclimb from there. Finally, there is an offwidth crack facing east near the left end of the rock. Rappel from a chockstone anchor (verify its reliability!) in the crack, and walk down the rest of the way.

17. Northeast Cutoff 7 Start in a vertical crack at the left end of the wall. After 15 feet, join an arching crack, and, as feasible, move to the upper right slanting crack (small stoppers). There is a large knob midway along the crack and beneath it. Continue along the crack, and make a blind faith jam as it joins the vertical hand crack forming the upper part of *Bad Saturday.* Belay in a niche below an offwidth (140 feet). Climb the offwidth to the top. This fine climb is 5.5 except for the runout 5.7 move prior to joining *Bad Saturday.*

18. Croissant 6 This alternative is a preferred start to *Kitchen's Delight.* Begin as for the preceding climb, but follow the crescent shaped crack below *Northeast Cutoff* until it intersects *Kitchen's Delight.*

19. Kitchen's Delight 7+ Start 7 yards to the right of *Northeast Cutoff* behind a big boulder. Climb an easy right leaning ramp. As the ramp ends, enter a vertical crack. Ascend 30 feet, and move right to a bolt belay. (Using the *Croissant* start, this is a 160 foot pitch.) Move right from the belay stance, climb along a right facing flake (big cams), and then traverse under an overhanging flake (crux--small cams) to a nice hand crack. Ascend that, and belay off the bolts to the right.

The CRYSTAL FREEWAY

17. Northeast Cutoff 7
19. Kitchen's Delight 7+
22. Bad Saturday 8-
24. Exit Ramp 11b
25. Flake Out 11a
26. Orange Christmas 11a
27. Grunt Layback 9
29. Strawberry Jam 8

GS

Figure 4.6

20. Change of Hand 9- Start on the crack at the beginning of *Bad Saturday,* but instead of traversing right at the crux flake, go left and continue up the slabs bearing slightly left. For all practical purposes this route is a solo, since there is the potential for an 80 foot fall at the crux. This climb is not recommended (a.k.a as *Change of Hard).*

21. Low Road 2 This insignificant line slants up below the overhang on the second pitch of *Kitchen's Delight.* It allows the indolent to avoid the second pitches of *Kitchen's Delight* and *Northeast Cutoff.*

22. Bad Saturday 8- Begin at a right facing, flake crack which ends after 20 feet. Traverse left to a larger right facing, flake crack forming a chimney. Ascend to a shelf. Then traverse right and lieback along the ever present flake (crux). Now climb to a low angle, right leaning crack and traverse right to a vertical crack joining *Northeast Cutoff* or *Kitchen's Delight.* An interesting climb.

23. Very Bad Saturday 11b An alternate start to *Bad Saturday.* Start at the beginning of *Bad Saturday.* Climb straight up a thin, hard to protect crack to rejoin *Bad Saturday.*

24. Exit Ramp 11b Find a dark water streak 45 yards left of *Orange Christmas.* Climb 15 feet of unprotected 9 friction to a short headwall, and clip a bolt which is just above the headwall and to the left of the water streak. Ascend straight to the next bolt, cross the water streak to the third bolt, and follow the remaining bolts to the belay station on a shelf on the left. Continue to the top following a line of bolts that are to the left of the belay station. This defiant route is sustained and occasionally runout.

25. Flake Out 11a This route ascends the prominent right facing dihedral in the middle of the face that opens into a 2 foot gap at the top. It can be approached by climbing the start of *Orange Christmas* or rappelling. The former creates a sensational, sustained climb at the 11a level.

26. Orange Christmas 11a Find an orange water streak behind a pine tree and 18 yards left of *Grunt Layback* dihedral. The first bolt on this route is just left of the water streak and 4 feet above the second horizontal seam. The second bolt is at 10:30 relative to the first bolt, while the 3rd bolt is 10 feet higher and slightly left. The crux comes early on this climb, and, while the upper section is mostly 7-8, it is very runout and the bolts are difficult to see. If done as one pitch, it is longer than 165 feet and requires simulclimbing which, considering the early crux, may not be desirable. It can be done in two pitches by setting a belay at the bottom of *Flake Out.* For those comfortable at 5.11, this is a very fine climb.

27. Grunt Layback 9 Seven yards left of *Strawberry Jam* is a right facing dihedral that arches over to join *Strawberry Jam*. Tiptoe up to the crack (exposed 8). Whether you jam or lieback from then on, the quantity of grunting remains fixed. An elegant, virile climb.

28. Paul Piana Has A Need To Be Famous 9 Mr. Piana has satisfied his need in more elegant and distinguished ways than the title of this portmanteau climb. Start *Grunt Layback* and go left at a crack about 40 feet up. Belay near here to avoid rope drag on the next pitch. Move left along the crack and left onto the face, looking for the hard to see bolts on *Orange Christmas* positioned at 10:30 and 1:00. Go slightly right and exit. The last pitch is 5.7 and very runout.

29. Strawberry Jam 8 The name describes the thighs of those who wear shorts on this route. Begin in a hand crack towards the right end of the wall. The crack starts in a right facing dihedral which, after about 40 feet, suddenly turns into an offwidth. Climb all the way to an alcove formed by the left wall and an overhanging rock (125 feet of stiff, sustained 5.8). Belay. The next pitch of low 5th class ascends a short offwidth and traverses left to the rappel station. This route is a peach of a climb.

SOUTHWEST SIDE

The next two climbs will be found far around on the southwest side of Friction Tower towards its left end. There is a small spire (Gill Spire) at the right (west) end of the northwest side of the Tower. Rumor has it that there is a 5.7 route up the spire put in by John Gill in the 70's. The next climb starts down to the left (west) in front of the southwest side of the spire.

30. Strong Love 11b Climb the 25 foot thin hand crack splitting a large block. It first leans left and then right.

31. Mr. Chimp 12b There is a large overhanging boulder right of the Gill Spire on the southwest side of Friction Tower. This route starts just right of the overhang. Climb a right leaning thin finger crack (11) to a flared horizontal crack. Traverse right a few feet (crux) to a vertical crack. Continue up it (11) to a shelf.

OLD EASY

The many featured face of Old Easy (Figs. 4.7-8) rises up to the northeast of the upper climbers' parking lot. Major orientation features are as follows. Straight ahead you can see a large roof on the left side of the south face. *MRC Direct* is a straight up crack just left of the roof. It starts about 100 feet below the roof, passes the roof on the left, and continues on in a trough. *The Straight Edge,* a fist crack, starts just above and to the right of the finish of *MRC Direct* and reaches to the skyline. The semicircular crack on *Golden Grief* is visible to the right of the middle of the *MRC Direct. Colostemmy*, a wide V-shaped chimney, is visible near the right end of the wall.

MRC COMPLEX

To approach *MRC Direct,* hike up the gully below the right side of the roof, and then work left following the path of least resistance. If any real technical climbing is encountered, you're off route. There are rappel bolts on top of the mound left of the finish of *MRC Direct.* The rappel can be done using one or two ropes. Two ropes gets you to the ground. A one rope rappel from the top leads to a rappel stance at the end of the first pitch of *MRC Direct.* The distance is 82 feet and ends on an exposed, sloping shelf! You can also descend from the *MRC* routes by downclimbing *Left Exit.*

The next two routes are about 100 yards below the very right end of the roof on *MRC Direct.* They are on a slabby arete facing 110°. Descend by walking off.

32. Gehe Jetzt 8 This ancient line starts on either of the two wide cracks below the arete. At the top of the cracks traverse a little to the left, climb a fist crack to the arete, and follow it to the top.

33. Arrêtez Maintenant 9 Follow a bolt line up the arete, move left onto the face, and follow more bolts to rejoin the arete (a.k.a. *Old Easy Arete*).

By mixing and matching the routes described below you can choose your own path of ascent for the various MRC options.

34. MRC Direct 9 This is a true classic, especially when combined with *The Straight Edge.* Start up a tricky, wide cleft filled with vertical flakes forming finger and hand cracks. Continue until a small horizontal section is reached. Move slightly right, and power up a hand jam (8+) to a little shelf below the roof. Belay at the bolts. Pitch 2 fires straight over the roof, or first climbs to a shelf on the left and then rejoins the crack--alternatives of equal difficulty. After a couple of difficult moves above the roof, the climbing eases off for the next 50 feet. Belay on the big

The **MRC** Complex

rap

36

37

44

42

43

41

BIG
ROOF

Golden
Triangle

34. MRC Direct 9
36. Middle Exit 9
37. Straight Edge 9+
39. Right Start 7+
40. Far Right Start 7+
41. Seam Variation 10c
42. MRC Left 7
43. Finger Trip 10a
44. Ralph Called 10a

39

40

34

32, 33

Figure 4.7

shelf at the base of the exit pitches. At this point the following options are available: rappel; downclimb *Left Exit;* (recommended) climb *Middle Exit* or *The Straight Edge.*

35. Left Exit 4 Hike up the gully left of *MRC Direct.* Turn right towards a cleft (facing 320°) formed against the back wall, and climb it.

There are two ways to descend from the next two climbs. Climb a small wall to the left, walk (exposed) towards *Left Exit,* and carefully step down on a little shelf and then onto a boulder in the chimney. From here either descend the chimney or take the rappel exit for *MRC Direct.* Alternatively, scramble to the right past the base of *Buttox.*

36. Middle Exit 9 Step over an exciting 2 foot gap into the wide crack on the left (protectable with a small camming unit in the flake on the right). Move up the off-width to the bulge (crux) which can be taken straight in on good hand jams. Nothing smaller than #3.5 Friend plus some stoppers for the belay.

37. The Straight Edge 9+ Again, step over the exciting gap, this time towards the hand/fist crack on the right (RP or small camming unit). Then move into the crack, and jam up to the little niche. The next 10 feet of strenuous jamming are the crux. Two #4 Friends and a #4 Camalot come in handy here. Medium to large stoppers for the belay anchor (a.k.a. *The Right Exit*).

38. Left Start 5 Climb the chimney that is left of the start of *MRC Direct.* Then traverse right until rejoining *MRC Direct* at the start of the hand jam, or continue right to join the next route.

39. Right Start 7+ Move 7 yards right from the base of *MRC Direct* along a shelf. Climb up a bottomed out seam for 10 feet to another shelf. Use a flake to surmount the little headwall, climb past a bolt, and join *MRC Direct* near the start of the second pitch. The protection is poor on this route.

40. Far Right Start 7+ Fifteen yards past the preceding route is another crease. Climb it to the shelf and traverse left to join *Right Start* below the bolt. Poor protection.

41. Seam Variation 10c This looks like a great line, but the protection is skimpy at the start (crux) and the crack collects dirt higher up. Instead of entering the jam crack on the first pitch of *MRC Direct,* step left and climb the left slanting crack. RP's and strong fingers are needed at the start.

42. MRC Left 7 Great for photo-ops as well as climbing. The roof looks 10 but isn't. At the end of the first pitch of *MRC Direct,* do an easy traverse left to a prominent vertical crack, and belay. Fire over the bucket filled roof above, and continue on to the end of the crack.

43. Finger Trip Roof 10a A more challenging, but less elegant way to get over the roof on *MRC Direct*. Start at the belay stance at the end of the first pitch of *MRC Direct*. Traverse right 10 feet and make a blind jam into a crack (psychological crux). Then climb over the roof (crux), and after a few feet rejoin *MRC Direct*.

44. Ralph Called 10a Half way up the second pitch of *MRC Direct,* a thin, lichenous crack rises up vertically on the left. Using artful protection, ascend it to a bolt on the face above. Climb to a bolt 15 feet higher and then on to the rappel station. This is a fine alternative ending to the second pitch of *MRC Direct,* since it offers challenging climbing instead of low fifth class--but it's runout. You can traverse onto the face of this route by sneaking in from the left about two thirds of the way up *MRC Left.*

45. Mountaineers Rock Climb 9 This is the original *MRC*. Climb *Left Start* to *Right Start* with a belay along the way. Then climb to the base of *MRC Left* and belay. Foot traverse right along the shelf to *MRC Direct,* and enter it above the crux overhang. This last move was originally done on aid. If so, the route rates 5.7 A1.

46. Train Leaves at 7 7 This route uses an alternative second pitch to *Mountaineers Rock Climb.* Climb *MRC Left* rather than traversing right into *MRC Direct*. This climb yields the only MRC ascent to the top with no move harder than 5.7.

GOLDEN TRIANGLE

For the next 3 climbs, hike the gully as for *MRC* but do not veer left until approximately at the height of the start of the climbs. *No Name Chimney* and *Dire Pitch* are moderate chimneys (Fig. 4.8) with a history of being used for training. They still serve that purpose admirably for a new generation of climbers whose all around skills may lag behind their agility at clipping bolts. The traditional rating for these two climbs is 5.6.

47. No Name Chimney 7 There are two flaky chockstones at the beginning of this wide crack. About 50 feet up, a hand crack forms on the left wall as the climbing steepens (crux). Continue to a terrace and belay. Proceed up parallel hand cracks leading to the last belay on *MRC Direct.*

48. Dire Pitch 8 This route starts 17 yards farther uphill from *No Name Chimney* in a corner formed by a left facing dihedral. The crack varies in width. There is a rectangular capstone 80 feet up. Climb to a platform below the capstone (7) and belay. Squeeze past the capstone on the left (8--going right is 9+) out onto the

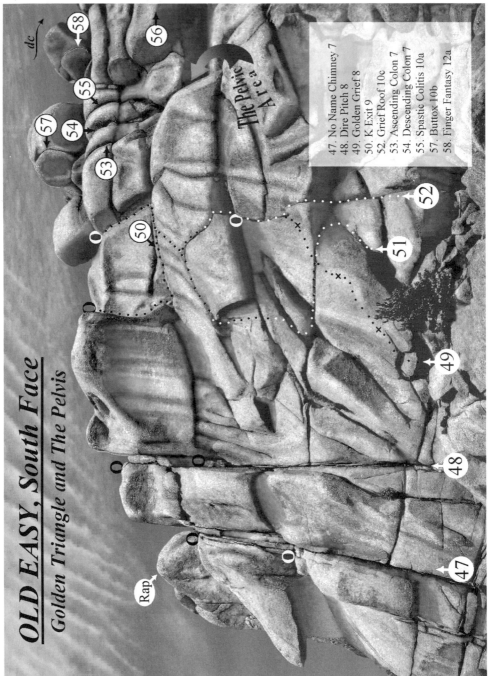

OLD EASY, South Face
Golden Triangle and The Pelvis

dc →

The Pelvic Area

47. No Name Chimney 7
48. Dire Pitch 8
49. Golden Grief 8
50. K Exit 9
52. Grief Roof 10c
53. Ascending Colon 7
54. Descending Colon 7
55. Spastic Colitis 10a
57. Buttox 10b
58. Finger Fantasy 12a

Rap

Figure 4.8

face near an ancient bolt. Then follow the crack to the top. Descent is by walk-down to the right.

Golden Grief starts 17 yards uphill from the preceding climb on a low angle face with 3 bolts. Descent is by downclimbing to the right and gradually working back to the base following the line of least resistance (or downclimb *Colostemmy*).

49. Golden Grief 8 Excellent variety. Start at the right of two cracks below the bolts, surmount a little headwall (distinctly harder for short climbers), and climb past the two bolts to a third bolt. Traverse low to a crack on the right. At the top of the crack (RP's and small Friends), move out right onto a cramped shelf (dis-tinctly harder for tall climbers), and belay. Do a tricky move to enter the left lean-ing crack on the left. The climbing eases up as the crack ends on an easy face leading to a belay on a shelf.

50. K Exit 9 About 30 feet before the end of *Golden Grief,* make an easy trav-erse left to the base of a big right facing dihedral. Climb the dihedral using me-dium gear, and exit on the right of an overhanging rock (large gear). Classic Vedauwoo 5.9.

51. Third Time Around 9 One time is more than enough. Walk to the right around the slab forming the start of *Golden Grief,* and struggle up left on an inside corner to gain the ledge between the 2nd and 3rd bolts of *Golden Grief.* Traverse left until below the left side of the semicircular crack on *Golden Grief.* Climb up to it, surmounting a small roof, and rejoin *Golden Grief.*

52. Grief Roof 10c A boulder problem start to *Golden Grief.* The crack at the end of the first pitch of *Golden Grief* extends below a roof. Start 10 feet below the roof, and climb the deceptively difficult crack to the roof. Struggle over the roof to rejoin *Golden Grief.*

THE PELVIS

About 35 yards uphill from *Golden Grief* is a blind hallway whose far end faces southeast. The hallway is a little left of *Colostemmy*. On its left side can be seen a hand crack and, just to its right, a chimney/offwidth. Looking straight above this section to an upper terrace, you can see a bulging rock split by the *Buttox* crack.

53. Ascending Colon 7 This is the hand crack mentioned above. Peristaltic mo-tion leads to *Buttox.*

54. Descending Colon 7 This is the chimney/offwidth which, if good form is not maintained, can result in propulsive descent.

55. Spastic Colitis 10a Start as for *Descending Colon,* but 20 feet up take the right leaning crack up to the headwall. Jog left 2 feet and pull over the headwall into the finger/hand crack.

56. Colostemmy 4 This is the large southwest facing chimney.

The next two climbs can be reached in several ways. The most obvious is to climb any of the preceding 4 routes. Alternately, one can climb *Golden Grief, Middle Exit* or *Straight Edge,* or hike up from the right end of the gully.

57. Buttox 10b Therapeutic handjamming for the anal retentive who need practice on overhanging cracks. Stoppers for the belay. Walkdown.

58. Finger Fantasy 12a The fantasy is this, Will you have any fingers left after the start of this climb? For the competent, this is a well protected, fun outing. This route is 12 yards right of *Buttox* and is formed by a flake on the left wall.

5. HOLDOUT

Holdout is a flat faced crag of unusually simple structure for Vedauwoo. It sits be-tween the main Central Area on the north and the Nautilus on the southeast. When viewed from the climbs in the Central Area, it appears to be contigu-ous with the Nautilus but actually lies a 100 yards to the north of it. From the Nautilus parking lot, ap-proach Holdout by following a trail that leads north-east. From the main campground one can head straight to the crag for routes on the northwest side.

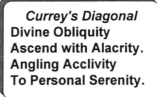

> *Currey's Diagonal*
> **Divine Obliquity**
> **Ascend with Alacrity.**
> **Angling Acclivity**
> **To Personal Serenity.**

For routes on the southeast side, go east from the end of the loop and then turn sharply left once past the first rock band. Holdout routes are generally fine, clean lines up faces that are unusually vertical by Vedauwoo standards.

SOUTHEAST SIDE

The singular orienting feature on this face is *Arch Stanton*. See Fig 5.1. Descend by down climbing *Up the Down Chimney* or rappel from bolts at the top of *Arch Stanton* or *Bushwhack Crack*. As long as the sun is out, this side is usually pleas-antly climbable since it's sheltered from the prevailing winds.

1. Through Thick and Thin 10a This climb begins 30 yards left of *Flaming Blue Jesus* and 8 yards left of the vertical gully described in the next route. Start in a 30 foot 5.8 offwidth crack in an open book whose left wall faces east. Continue to a roof. Pass it on the left via a hand crack (lesser crux), and belay on a ledge. Climb another 30 foot 5.8 offwidth to a ledge, and finish on a fist crack (crux). De-scend by climbing the last pitch of the next climb or by proceeding 3rd class to the right to get to the top of *Arch Stanton*.

2. Wright of Thick and Thin 7+ This climb originates in a 15 foot wide vertical gully located 22 yards left of *Arch Stanton*. Climb the wide crack on the left side of the gully. Stay in the crack until it ends (80 feet), and belay. The next two pitches are shorter and easier. Climb the little headwall in back of the belay, walk right about 10 feet, ascend a chimney, and belay on a ledge. The last pitch climbs a short, narrow crack in a right facing dihedral on the back wall. There are bolts at the top from which you can rappel to the northwest. Alternately, scramble to the top of *Arch Stanton,* and rappel from there.

Due to the lack of protection at the start of *Blue Jesus,* the next two climbs, both decent lines, do not get done often and may be weedy.

Southeast Side

HOLDOUT

1. Thick and Thin 10a
2. Wright of T & T 7+
3. Flaming Blue Jesus 10b
4. Mandella 11a
5. Arch Stanton 11d
6. Wide and Ugly 11a
7. Narrow and Ugly 8
8. Bushwhack 6
9. 19th Nervous Breakdown 9+
10. Existential Dilemma 8

Figure 5.1

3. Flaming Blue Jesus 10b Start at the base of *Arch Stanton,* and follow the crack formed by a right facing dihedral above a triangular boulder. This is best done as a top rope for a fall at the beginning will send you down in flames, as there is no real protection for the first 30 feet (crux). The climbing then eases up and gear can be placed, but by then who cares.

4. Mandela 11a This is a thin crack which veers off to the right, 30 feet from the top of the preceding route.

5. Arch Stanton 11d This stunning feature of Holdout's southeast wall is a popular hangout and occasionally even gets climbed. Forty feet of sustained, demanding underclings (11c) are followed by a crux exit up the face. A #2.5 Friend can supplement the bolts along the arch--although if you're strong enough to set it, you probably don't need it. (This was a former aid route, *Rejecter Ejecter.* Todd Skinner and Paul Piana led the first free ascent to near the end of the arch and renamed it *Arch Stanton.* Later, Piana completed the arch, freed the headwall, and renamed the climb *Terminator Blueprint* which, somehow or other, appeared in the literature as *Annihilator Blueprint.* However, Piana and Skinner's original choice so aptly described the line that the new names have never taken hold.)

6. Wide and Ugly 11a Beauty is in the eye of the belayer. The climb is pleasingly plump. Begin 35 yards right of the start of *Arch Stanton,* and jam up an overhanging hand to fist crack before hooking up with *Bushwhack.*

To reach the remaining climbs, go to the northeast end of the crag and scramble up a gully that faces east. There is a big horizontal flagstone to the left of the top of the gully. *Bushwhack* is 14 yards straight ahead.

7. Narrow and Ugly 8 A vertical finger crack arises 12 yards left of the start of *Bushwhack.* Climb the crack (crux) to the *Bushwhack* Ledge, traverse left a few feet, and climb the thin crack in the right facing dihedral just right of the *Bushwhack* exit.

8. Bushwhack 6 Climb a 10 foot high offwidth formed by a huge flake. Do a very easy traverse along a ledge and exit on a left slanting offwidth crack at the end of the ledge (may involve a move of 5.7).

9. 19th Nervous Breakdown 9+ Poor man's *Arch Stanton.* Start just right of *Bushwhack* in a crack that arches left, almost touching *Bushwhack,* before it finishes in a vertical crack. There are a couple of hard moves where the crack arches over (easier for tall people taking Prozac), and then it's casual going. It's nice as far as it goes, but it doesn't go far.

10. Up the Down Chimney 5 Three yards left of *Existential Dilemma* is a chimney facing east and lying between a huge flake and the main wall. This was the 3rd class descent route before the installation of rappel bolts It's now an ascent route. *Tempora mutantur nos et mutamer in illis!* (Times change and we change with them!)

11. Existential Dilemma 8 Upon completing the first ascent in 1951, Jean-Paul Sartre exclaimed: "Offwidths are not redeemable!" The course of twentieth century philosophy and climbing would have been far different, if he had only worn long pants. This route is the theological counterpoint to *Flaming Blue Jesus.* Begin in a slot near the top of the gully, move into a left facing dihedral (crux), follow the crack to the top, and then wonder if it was worth the effort in this meaningless universe.

NORTHWEST SIDE

Use the southeast side descent routes for the next 3 climbs. *Oslund's Delight, Beef Eater,* and *Currey's Diagonal* are the principal orienting structures on this side of Holdout. See Fig. 5.2.

12. Oslund's Delight 8 Hike up a platform at the very left end of the wall, and find a left facing dihedral above a pile of boulders. Make a tricky start off the boulders in order to enter the dihedral, and then enjoy some fine finger jamming to the top. There are two alternate starts that can turn this into a two pitch climb. Both begin on the ground below the platform where the climb proper starts. The first begins 12 yards left of the dihedral and is a short, pleasant hand crack that leads to the platform. The second, located directly below the dihedral, is a left sloping hand crack that leads to the regular start.

13. Rainbow in the Dark 11a This climb begins 16 yards to the right of the *Oslund's* dihedral in an inset between big boulders and on the same lower level as the alternate starts to *Oslund's*. Climb a finger crack to a ledge and then follow an arching overhang to the left. Protecting this climb takes considerable effort.

14. Reading Raymond Chandler 12a Begin at a huge flake 20 yards left of *Static Cling,* and ascend an extraordinarily thin, left leaning crack containing one piton.

15. Static Cling 11d Begin off a triangular flake 38 yards left of *Currey's Diagonal* and ascend a thin, left leaning, finger tip crack.

16. Currey's Diagonal 10b This is the imposing right slanting crack in the middle of the crag with a small tree about 30 feet up. Clip 2 pitons on the way to the tree. Once past the tree, the route goes at 5.9 to the rappel station. Gear: RP's , me-

Figure 5.2

dium stoppers, and small camming devices. This climb is guaranteed to give a joyful slant to your day. (This route illustrates nicely the change in climbing expectations over the years. The assumed time for an ascent in the mid-60's was 3½ hours and the rating was 5.8 A1.)

17. Eleven Cent Moon 11d Recommended. Below the top of *Currey's,* a left facing dihedral forms a crescent. A thin, left arching crack is below and right of the crescent. Ascend the crack going past a piton and aiming for the beginning of the crescent. Traverse as needed. Follow the crescent past three bolts supplemented by some small gear. **17a. Left Start Eleven Cent Moon 12a** There is an alternative, unprotected 12a start in a tiny right facing dihedral below the tip of the crescent.

18. Silver Surfer 9 Preclassic. The surf's never up on this one which doesn't go far, but it's fun while it lasts. Eleven yards left of *Beef Eater* is a crack formed on the right side of two big flagstones propped against the main wall. The crack faces 230˚, has a gap in the middle, is wide below the gap and narrow above it. Climb the crack and move right onto the wall for a few feet to rappel bolts. Small to medium gear suffices despite the wide start.

19. North Shore 13b Neoclassic. The surf's up on this one which probably goes further than you'd like along an uncompromisingly direct ride to the top. From the belay stance on *Silver Surfer,* follow a line of bolts up to the rappel bolts on the horizon just below which is the crux.

20. Pipeline 12a Postclassic. If you're too diffident to show off in *North Shore,* take this more casual ride. It angles up right from the belay stance on *Silver Surfer* and follows a series of weaknesses as it rises to rappel bolts on the horizon.

21. Beef Eater 10b Classic. Not for vegetarians or anti-royalists. Begin on a face to the right of a dihedral with a big roof. At the roof, hand traverse right (5.9) and pass the roof on the right. Belay on a shelf below the upper pitch--a classic hand to finger crack with rappel bolts at the top. Two #1 Friends and #2 Friends will make you feel like royalty on the second pitch. The first pitch is often avoided by traversing in from the right (exposed!). Since the first pitch offers good climbing, this is not recommended even though this was the path of the first ascent party who named the route *Ten Pin* (5.8 A1).

6. NAUTILUS

N autilus is the premier crag at Vedauwoo with over 100 established routes at all degrees of difficulty. Crack climbs predominate with a sprinkling of bolted faces and some sparkling mixed routes. This huge climbing wall, designed by Jules Verne, runs for a couple of hundred yards on a southwest to northeast axis. The north facing Parabolic Slab can be seen high atop the south section of the Nautilus soon after taking the Vedauwoo cutoff. To get to Nautilus, go a quarter mile past the Central Area Turnoff and turn left into a parking lot at the southwest end of the Nautilus. Looking up towards Nautilus you can see the steep, flat southwest face of the Ted's Trot Block which contains *Drunken Red Neck Rappelers, a* spectacular bolted face route. The crack to its left is *Finally.*

The routes will be described starting at the left end of the southeast side of Nautilus and proceed more or less counterclockwise around this complex promontory. Getting through the boulders can be complicated on the southeast side. Persistence and observation from 70 yards away from the cliff will help. Descent from all the routes from *Easy Jam* going counterclockwise through *Flying Buttress* is by walkdown on the north side of the southwest end of the Nautilus. Go right of *Finally* and left of

> *Flying Buttress 10b* ... si-**multaneously executed crack, chimney, and face moves synchronized with precise exploitation of the back wall.**

Stand and Deliver. If you climb to a route finishing on top of Ted's Trot Block, you can rappel from there to join this descent.

THREE SISTERS

The first group of climbs is found in the Three Sisters Amphitheater (Fig. 6.1). Short routes -- they make good practice and toprope ascents. To get to the Amphitheater walk right from the parking lot along a faint trail to the southeast side of Nautilus. As you come abreast of Ted's Trot Block, head into the boulders (11:00) eventually walking through a portal with a flat, slanting roof onto a slab. From there enter the Amphitheater from its right side. A flange, forming a bottomed out crack on a wall facing 40°, is found at the far left end of the amphitheater.

1. Ejector-Rejector 10a Lieback the crack. Nice toprope problem--no protection.

2. Slut 7 Start a yard to the right of the preceding route in a slightly opened book crack that veers to the right after 8 feet. Follow it to the top.

Figure 6.1 The Three Sisters Area

3. Folded, Spindled, and Mutilated 10a Begin a yard to the right of *Slut* in a crack with a handle in it. Follow it to the ledge. The name goes back to the time when IBM punched cards were common and were to be handled with care. Take care of yourself, and toprope this one--the rock is friable.

4. Slat 7 and 4a. Tat Exit 10a The best climb in this group. An arm's length away from *Route 3* is a right leaning crack in a right facing dihedral. Climb past the crux start to a platform and go left and ascend a low angle ramp using a left leaning crack in a left facing dihedral. The *Tat Exit* avoids this last crack by climbing straight ahead up a thin, vertical crack in a right facing dihedral (this is the left of the two thin cracks above the platform). Take a #3.5 or #4 Friend for the surprise ending.

5. Little Stone 11a Four yards left of *Slit,* a thin slanting line with a bit of a lip angles towards *Slat.* This route has actually been led using RP's, but it's best regarded as a high boulder problem.

6. Slit 7 There is a wide chimney at the right end of the alcove. Climb it (5.5--no protection for 20 feet) to a large shelf, and continue up the offwidth above. Using the flakes on the right while climbing the offwidth is called *Layne Variation.*

7. Slick and Superficial 12c There is a vertical wall just right of the amphitheater containing a bottomed out crack that ends after 20 feet. Work out the desperate boulder start to the crack and, with minimal protection, climb it. Clip the bolt on the left, and make a heinous traverse to the crack on the left. Follow it to the top, and enjoy the easier climbing.

There is an enclosed nook 3 yards to the right of *Slick and Superficial.* Its front (southeast) side is composed of two large, rather flat, vertical boulders with a wide crack between them.

8. Petite Tarsalation 3 This climb starts in the nook proper just left of the wide crack. Climb a hand crack while using the wide crack as convenient. Nice practice for beginning hand jammers. Descent: walkoff to the right (northeast)

9. Tarsalation 6 This is the offwidth/chimney crack on the front side of the two aforementioned boulders. It provides more good practice but no protection until near the exit. A toprope can be set up from the preceding climb.

SOUTHEAST SIDE, LEFT END

See Fig. 6.2 for an overview of this area. There is a ledge below the southeast face of Ted's Trot Block. Look to that part of the ledge below the right end of the block. Two offwidth cracks can be seen below this section. They are separated by

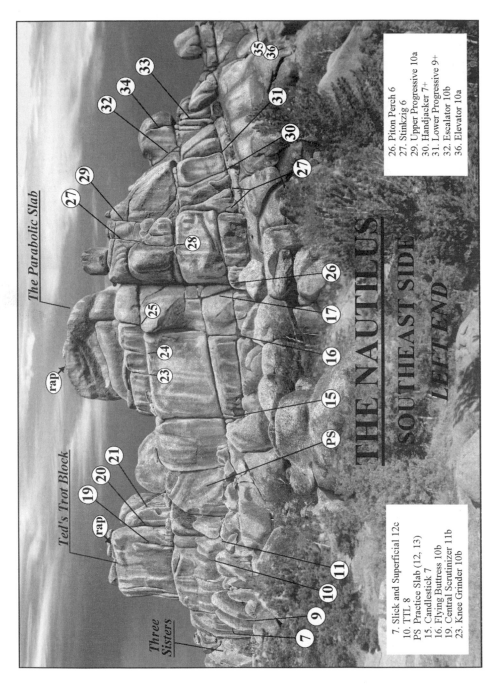

The Parabolic Slab

Ted's Trot Block

Three Sisters

THE NAUTILUS
SOUTHEAST SIDE
LEGEND

7. Slick and Superficial 12c
10. TTL 8
PS Practice Slab (12, 13)
15. Candlestick 7
16. Flying Buttress 10b
19. Central Scrutinizer 11b
23. Knee Grinder 10b

26. Piton Perch 6
27. Stinkzig 6
29. Upper Progressive 10a
30. Handjacker 7+
31. Lower Progressive 9+
32. Escalator 10b
36. Elevator 10a

Figure 6.2

a 6 foot wide tongue of rock at the top and a molar shaped rock at the start. Puzzle your way through the boulders below to get there. The left offwidth is *TTL,* and the right one is *TTR.*

10. TTL 8 This is a nice consistent climb with a spacious shelf in the middle.

11. TTR 6 A slightly easier version of the preceding climb.

There is a broad slab facing 120° about 35 yards to the right of *TTR.* It's called The Practice Slab (PS). On it will be found two lines of bolts leading to the top. These are superb leads for beginning climbers, good one handed exercises for more experienced climbers, and no handed exercises for the distinguished. The chimney behind PS also contains excellent training climbs which at this time are unprotected.

12. Etude For The Left Hand 5 Climb up the left route.

13. Etude For The Right Hand 5 Climb up the right route.

14. Practice Chimney 4-6 This is a wide chimney with many possible paths of ascent. It is directly behind the face of The Practice Slab (toprope--no protection).

To the right of The Practice Slab is a huge block. At its right end, a chimney leads to the main shelf at a point below the left edge of the Parabolic Slab.

15. Candlestick 7 Without subtle technique you could get burnt on the offwidth and chimney moves. Climb to the top of the chimney, move to the back wall and make a fun escape through an embrasure. Protection: #3-#4 Big Bros for the chimney; #4 Camalot and stoppers for exit.

16. Flying Buttress 10b Stupendous. Pitch 2 is arguably the best single pitch of 5.10 at Vedauwoo. Stop thinking and your butt will be flying. This ascent involves simultaneously executed crack, chimney, and face moves synchronized with precise exploitation of the back wall. Bring all Friends, #4 Camalot, and a sparse, widely spaced set of stoppers. The route is easily identified by its second pitch which is a great arching overhanging crack formed in a dihedral corner. Pitch 1 ascends the wide crack (8) below the arch leading to a large shelf with a fixed pin. The second pitch ascends the arching crack and finishes with a few easy offwidth moves to the ledge below *Hemoglobin.*

17. Flying Right 9+ This is a good climb on its own as well as an alternate first pitch for the preceding route (more in keeping with the character of its second pitch). Start a yard left of *Piton Perch,* and follow a leaning hand crack that blossoms into a triangular gap leading to the shelf at the start of the 2nd pitch of *Flying Buttress.*

The next group of climbs starts at the southwest corner of the Nautilus on the ledge supporting Ted's Trot Block. *Rappelers* is on the wall of Ted's Trot Block facing 210° and is shown in Fig. 6.11.

18. Drunken Redneck Rappelers 12a This beautifully positioned route is a sobering prospect that might well convince climbers to become sport rappelers. On the right side of the face, a stick clip bolt is the first in a line that leads to the top. Some small gear can be gotten in along the way.

Move around the corner to the right. The next route will be found there near the right end of the southeast face of Ted's Trot Block. It is just above TTL.

19. The Central Scrutinizer 11b Begin in a crack that contains a small pillar near the start. The crack disappears after 20 feet whereupon, *mirabile dictu,* 3 bolts appear on the right. Even more of a miracle is required to flash this sustained and varied route which occupies a splendid position.

20. Deep Throat 10a This is a deep, open book just around the corner from the preceding route. It starts wide and ends with a hand crack crux. If you practice safe climbing (RP's to #4 Camalot), this route can provide a satisfying experience in stemming.

21. Bombay 8 The open slot on the wall facing 50° and the worst climb at Vedauwoo--tape your belly for it. Worth doing once, to say you've done it. If you do it twice, you'll have a first--the first person to have ever climbed it twice. Protection: none if done straight up; if approached from the right some small gear can be placed in the next route. Landing: jumbled boulders.

22. Bombs Away 9+ Just right of *Bombay* is a thin crack system that offers diverse paths to the top. Choose one.

The next 3 short climbs are to the right of the open gap formed between the Ted's Trot prominence and the Parabolic Slab. They are short, not quite boulder problems, with *Hemoglobin* being the only one worth roping up for. Descent is from rappel slings to the left.

23. Knee Grinder 10b Five yards left of *Blood Sport* is a short crack with a miserable knee jam. Alternative: to achieve similar damage to your knees do squats with double your body weight.

24. Blood Sport 11c Seven yards left of *Hemoglobin* is a shallow finger crack in a small right facing dihedral. It's best regarded as a high boulder problem. Alternative: to achieve similar damage to your body engage in bull fighting without a cape.

25. Hemoglobin 8 This hand/finger crack is in a left facing dihedral and directly above *Flying Buttress*. Alternative: to achieve a similar physiological experience donate a pint of blood (actually, climb is OK; name antedates the practice of taping).

The following climbs are at the lower level of the rock band. The descent for the next 4 climbs is as the same as for *Mother #1* or *Escalator.*

26. Piton Perch 6 This deep chimney is below the right edge of the Parabolic Slab and splits the Nautilus. Ascend it thoughtfully getting past a chockstone near the top (crux).

27. Stinkzig 6 Highly recommended. Walk 30 yards uphill from *Piton Perch* to a large chimney facing southeast and formed by two huge blocks on the left and a spike and a tongue shaped rock on the right. You can start directly up the chimney, but a preferred start is to walk right and enter by the east facing breach between the spike and tongue. In any event, ascend the crack and belay on the shelf on the right. Step left across a gap, and climb the nice handcrack formed by a left facing dihedral. Turn sharply right at its end and climb another crack to the top. Except for one or two well protected moves of 5.7 on the first pitch, this neat climb is mostly 5.5.

28. Zigzag 10a From end of the first pitch of *Stinkzig,* scramble left along an exposed ledge. Continue all the way around the corner to a wide hand crack in a right facing, dihedral corner. Pull into the crack (crux) ,and set a belay before the start of the final handcrack in *Stinkzig.* Turn left onto a northeast facing wall, surmount some ledges at their weakness, and finish on easy face.

29. Upper Progressive 10a A funky, worthwhile climb that ascends the crack in the dihedral directly above the first pitch of *Stinkzig.* After an unsettling 20 feet the crack widens and overhangs. Get past this (crux) and enjoy the rest of it. Rack: through a #4 Camalot.

30. Handjacker 7+ Climb the crack on the right side of the glossal rock referred to in *Stinkzig.* A fine offwidth practice climb. Descent: Walk around the shelf to the right and downclimb the chimney below *Escalator.*

31. Lower Progressive 9+ Designated climb for Boulder political ascensionists. There is a wall facing 80° five yards right of *Handjacker*. There is an inclined hand crack in a dihedral corner at the right end of the wall. This is a minor classic with sustained, solid jamming, interesting face moves, and good protection. Rack: Sparse, widely spaced set of stoppers, all Friends, and a #4 Camalot for the exit. Finish on *Upper Progressive* or *Escalator,* or descend as for *Handjacker.*

32. Escalator 10b From the top of the preceding climb, scramble right to a southeast facing wall which contains a left leaning crack. The climb starts in a vertical crack leading to the oblique crack. For shorter climbers, gaining the obliqueness is the crux. Descend from rappel slings around the base of a rock about 15 feet above the belay stance.

33. Bat Heaven 10c There are two 35 foot vertical cracks a few feet apart just right of the bottom of the descent chimney below *Escalator.* The left one is filled with bat guano and the right one ought to be. Get a rabies shot and climb the right one.

34. Caesar 12d This is the thin seam above *Bat Heaven*--a toprope problem. It has not been led yet.

Looking 50 or so yards right from *Lower Progressive*, you can see a lower, relatively level, stretch of rock along the profile of Nautilus. There are four distinct large boulders towards the right end of the level stretch and a drop-off past the rightmost boulder. *Elevator* is the crack facing 60° formed in a dihedral corner by the leftmost of these boulders. To the left and in front of *Elevator* is *Step Ladder*, a chimney/offwidth crack. It starts and finishes at approximately the same level as *Elevator.* Descend by downclimbing the chimney between the two climbs.

35. Step Ladder 6 Squeeze in and up. Good warm up for the next climb.

36. Elevator 10a It arches over at the top where the going is a bit tricky. Otherwise, good solid jams all the way.

SOUTHEAST SIDE, RIGHT END

See Fig. 6.3 for this area. A trail starts about 20 yards out from the cliff and right of *Elevator.* Walking along the trail (counterclockwise relative to Nautilus), you will come to a large boulder with a pine tree growing from its northeast side. Farther ahead is a 12 foot high mushroom boulder directly behind which is a recessed area in the main wall. *Knothole* is in this recess.. Descent from the climbs from *Knothole* to *Crankenstine* is by walkoff to the left (southwest).

37. Knothole 8 A left leaning crack in a left leaning slot goes at low fifth class to a platform. The chimney to offwidth crack above is the crux. Just left of the start is a thin seam leading to a flake after 10 feet. This boulder problem (11) has been

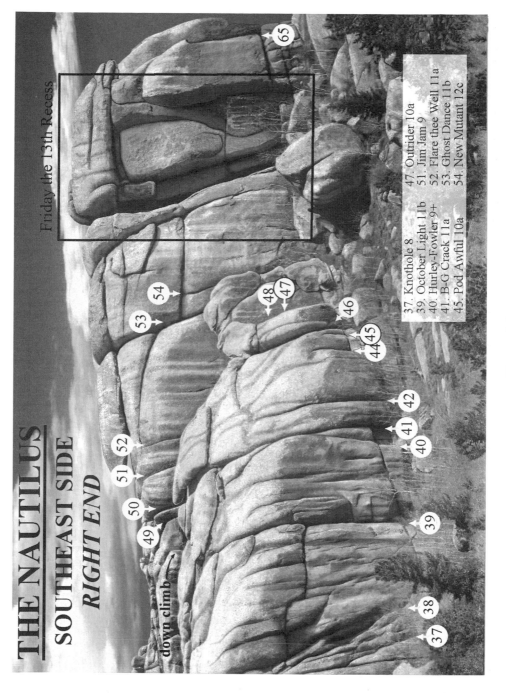

Figure 6.3

THE NAUTILUS
SOUTHEAST SIDE
RIGHT END

Friday the 13th Recess

down climb

37. Knothole 8
39. October Light 11b
40. Hurley-Fowler 9+
41. B-G Crack 11a
45. Pod Awful 10a

47. Outrider 10a
51. Jim Jam 9
52. Flare thee Well 11a
53. Ghost Dance 11b
54. New Mutant 12c

called *Pring Fever* or, less correctly, *Knothole Direct.*

38. Popcorn Farce 9+ Begin five yards right of *Knothole*. Climb up a deep, easy trough facing east that steepens, narrows, and becomes more difficult before moving right to another trough (crux #1). Belay on a ledge. Climb the crack above (crux #2) formed by a left facing dihedral. Maintain your composure on the subtle moves lest your climbing become farcical.

39. October Light 11b This super test piece is 20 yards right of *Popcorn Farce*. It's hands to offwidth through four overhanging bulges. Redpoint this, and you'll see the light. Gear: lots!

40. Hurley-Fowler 9+ This route begins 17 yards right of *October Light* in a right leaning slot with a chockstone twenty feet up. The crack narrows above the chockstone and tilts left. The intimidating aspect of this fine pitch keeps it from being climbed very often so that it collects vegetation. Take heart, enjoy, and help out with some gardening.

41. B-G Crack 11a Two yards right of *Hurley-Fowler* is a ceiling that's about 12 feet long. Starting on the left, traverse under the ceiling until you're beneath a crack that leans slightly left. Surmount the ceiling to enter the crack (uncrux). Climb the crack to the top. A wide section just past the beginning of the crack is the crux.

42. Crankenstine 11d Start five yards right of *B-G Crack* and in front of some aspen trees. Climb to a very thin crack that starts above guano covered ledges. There is a single bolt near the start of the crack. The climbing eases up after twenty feet. If the aspen trees are used, the climb is called *Frankenstine* and is easier (11b). Given the condition of the ledges, using a ladder is the best way to start.

There is a huge boulder containing a right slanting hand crack about 20 yards farther along the trail mentioned above. The boulder is on the trail and several yards away from the main wall.

43. Das Boot 10c Climb the slanting crack.

To descend from the routes from *Black and Decker* to *Hamburger Crack* walk back (northeast) until there is a sloping ramp facing east. Scramble down it to the base of *Ghost Dance*.

44. Black and Decker 11a This climb begins 10 yards right of *Crankenstine* in an open book corner containing a finger crack. As the crack ends, it arches left. Start climbing by making an exposed hand traverse from the right to gain the crack.

Climb the crack, continue to a bolt on the left, and then ascend the vertical water streak (crux) just past it. Sustained, varied climbing.

45. Pod Awful 10a Seven yards right of *Black and Decker* is a slot facing 70°. Traverse in from the right (exciting), ascend the slot, and finish on the slab above which is runout but never harder than 5.7. It's important to face the correct way in the offwidth start to the slot. This route is an easier version of the preceding one.

46. W.C.Fields 7 This impressive chimney is 5 yards right of *Pod Awful* and lies between a huge slab and the main wall. Traverse in from the right. For a chimney this route has reasonable protection. #4 Friend to #4 Big Bro's can be set as well as a medium piece in a horizontal crack near the start. About half way up is a hand crack that is not used in an obvious way.

Proceed around the corner to the right to a wall facing 40°. The next two routes are associated with this wall.

47. Outrider 10a Three bolts on the right side of the wall lead up a water streak in vague sort of way. Go left at the end to a belay stance. Small gear is useful at the top. Neat climb although the first bolt is a bit high up.

48. Hamburger Crack 7 This chimney is just right of *Outrider*. Good climbing and good view as you watch the lightly clad boys and girls on *Outrider,* but there's no protection until near the top.

The following 4 crack climbs are found on the southeast facing wall on the right (northwest) of the descent ramp described above. This is the same wall that contains *Ghost Dance*. A deep trough is formed between the ramp and the wall. The next four crack climbs start in the trough.

49. Jim Jam Junior 7 High up on the wall is a 30 foot finger of rock. Climb the offwidth crack on the left side of the finger. After a few technical moves of offwidth, the climbing moderates.

50. Joke 6 This is the hand crack on the right side of the finger.

51. Jim Jam 9 This seemly hand crack is 8 yards right of *Joke*.

52. Flare Thee Well 11a Worthwhile. Six yards right of *Jim Jam* is a left leaning finger crack. It protects OK with small gear in the hands of the competent.

53. Ghost Dance 11b Very fine climb. It's located to the right of *Flare Thee Well* and past the end of the downclimb slab. It starts behind a huge block. Climb up between the block and the wall. Then fire up a left leaning crack--hands to fist to an easy offwidth exit. A #4 Friend can be set soon after starting the crack with its crux entry moves. A full rack is useful, so you may wish to do this in two pitches to lighten the load. Descend by wandering left.

54. New Mutant 12c Beyond very fine. Seven yards right of *Ghost Dance* is a finger tip version of the same. It requires great competence to set protection, let alone climb this route. Rappel bolts 60 feet up.

FRIDAY THE 13TH RECESS

The Friday the 13th recess is 30 yards right of the last climb (Fig. 6.4). It's easily identifiable by the large chimney splitting it in two. There is a broad wall facing 80° on the left side of the recess. Two good routes are found on this wall. There is a rappel station at the top of *War Zone.* As a two rope rappel, it reaches the ground. Using one rope requires some easy downclimbing in *H&H Grunt.*

55. War Zone 11b Climb up along cracks in the center of the face. A little past half way up, you come to a line of bolts that protects the crux finish. A less preferred start climbs to the bulge in *Deception* and then goes left to join the bolts.

56. Deception 9 This climb has become more popular in recent years, perhaps due to its proximity to *Friday the 13th* and *War Zone.* Start by climbing the cracks that angle left from just left of the chimney. Mostly 5.5 with a touch of 5.7. An optional belay can be set up on a sloping ledge. Climb past a slightly overhanging bulge to a hand crack on the right in a dihedral corner. This leads to a short chimney exit with a belay on a flat platform. Descent options: (i) climb up the back wall (10 feet of unprotected 5.8) to get to the rappel bolts on *War Zone*; (ii) downclimb to the right and then wander off to the left; (iii) downclimb *H&H Grunt.*

57. H&H Grunt 6 Climb is better than the name. Recommended. Start by heading towards the *Deception* dihedral using a crack slightly right of the *Deception* crack. Just below the dihedral move right into the chasm and belay on an enclosed platform. (Alternately, you can arrive at this point by squeezing through a chimney behind a flake and the right wall.) Gaze up right to a large chimney structure. Make an exciting step right towards the structure entering a slot with double cracks. At its top, step right into the *Thin Man* chimney (crux) and belay on top. Rappel from bolts atop *Middle Parallel Space.*

Friday the 13th, a real masterpiece, is on the right side of the recess. It's a stunning straight in hand crack splitting two big roofs as it goes from the bottom to the top of the crag. For all practical purposes it's 5 different climbs: pitch 1 (10a), pitch 2 (11a), pitch 3 (11d), *Part II* (11a), and *Friday Blues* (11d and sustained).

58. Friday the 13th 11d Perform a boulder move or two of 10a lieback in the thin crack which then widens to hands and steady 5.8/9 for 60 feet. The pitch

FRIDAY THE 13th RECESS
55. War Zone 11b 59. Fri 13th, Part 2, 11a
56. Deception 9 60. Hesit. Blues 11b
57. H & H Grunt 6 61. Mid. Par. Space 9
58. Friday the 13th 11d 62. Air Voyager 12b

Figure 6.4

Figure 6.5 Steve Bechtel going ballistic on the top roof of
Friday the 13th (11d)

ends at bolts below the roof. Options at this point are: rappel; traverse left and climb *Friday the 13th, Part II;* climb pitch 2. To climb the 2nd pitch struggle out right over the roof to the next set of bolts below the top ceiling. Rappel, or continue on to pitch 3. To climb pitch 3 move left past a flange and fire through the crack on the top roof. Rappel from bolts atop *Middle Parallel Space.*

59. Friday the 13th, Part II 11a This is an excellent, alternative finish for *Friday the 13th.* At the end of the first pitch of that route, make a delicate hand traverse left (11a--small RP's) to the crack formed by two big chockstones, and jam it to the *Deception* belay -- 10d, good protection, and a tingly 60 feet of air below.

60. Hesitation Blues 11b This climb starts around the corner to the right of *Friday the 13th* in a thin crack at the left side of a broad flake. Jam and lieback the crack until the line arches over and belay at a bolt. Pitch 2 ascends to the roof via a stridently vertical hand crack in a dihedral corner. Go left to the belay of the second pitch of *Friday the 13th,* or go right and exit on *Middle Parallel Space.* The only flaw in this wonderful climb is questionable protection at the start due to crunchy rock.

If the none of the above satisfies you, try *Friday Blues 11d, the* hardwoman tour -- *Hesitation Blues* followed by pitch 3 of *Friday the 13th.* This yields three sustained pitches of 5.11 climbing.

THE PROW

The northeast end of the crag, encompassing the routes from *Right Parallel Space* to *Gravity's Rainbow,* is known as The Prow of the Nautilus (Fig. 6.8). The Prow begins at the far right end of the southeast side of Nautilus in an area dominated by a huge 75 foot high flake forming a giant shield in front of the main wall. A vast chimney is behind the shield. You can use the bolts atop *Middle Parallel Space,* or at the end of its first pitch, to descend from routes on The Prow. We include *Middle Parallel Space* and *Grand Traverse* in this section for ease of description.

61. Middle Parallel Space 9 True classic--two pitches of sustained diverse climbing. There is a crack in the dihedral formed by the left side of the shield and the main wall. Struggle up this crack for 25 feet of hand/fist jamming (9) to a platform. Continue up the now hand sized crack using the shield for a comfortable back rest . Thirty feet up from the platform, stem out to the top of the shield for a bolt belay. Climb back into the crack, traverse right at its end, and surmount the ceiling (8+) where there is a small crack through it. Climb straight up unprotected 5.7 for 15 feet to belay/rappel bolts, or go right a little and up easier rock.

Figure 6.6 Climbers on the second pitch of *Hesitation Blues* (11b)

**Figure 6.7 Scott Blunk -- your typical *Air Voyager with Report* (12b).
Photograph courtesy of Piana/Cowboyography**

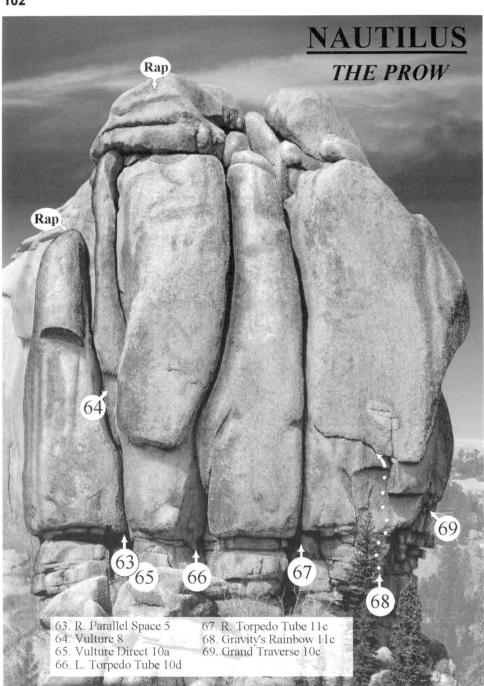

NAUTILUS
THE PROW

63. R. Parallel Space 5
64. Vulture 8
65. Vulture Direct 10a
66. L. Torpedo Tube 10d
67. R. Torpedo Tube 11c
68. Gravity's Rainbow 11c
69. Grand Traverse 10c

Figure 6.8

62. Air Voyager With Report 12b Buy flight insurance before climbing. A great route despite (because of ?) the epoxy reinforced holds. Same start as the preceding route but follow the bolts up the right face of the dihedral. The runout near the crux top has produced many Frequent Flier Points.

The right side of the shield contains an awesome, east facing Y shaped cavity.

63. Right Parallel Space 5 An esthetic, spacious chimney with a beautiful view over the plains. It's runout most of the way since parallel lines never meet. Start at the bottom of the cavity, and climb left in the huge chimney behind the shield. Set a #4 Camalot and scale 20 unprotected feet to an old bolt and another unprotected 20 feet to the top.

64. Vulture 8 This is an alternate and inferior start to the next climb. Begin at *Right Parallel Space* and veer right to *Vulture Direct.* Short climbers and the inflexible may think the climb is harder than 8.

65. Vulture Direct 10a This fine crack climb (orientation 140°) has an early crux near the pinch off. Start on the right side of the cavity in an obvious hand crack that becomes a stemming problem after 25 feet. Exit on *Middle Parallel Space.*

The gaping, overhanging start to the next climb lies 5 yards right of *Vulture Direct.*

66. Left Torpedo Tube 10d A real test piece for the offwidth aficionado. The crux is the sustained, overhanging start. The final vertical section is 5.8-9 offwidth. Rack: #3.5 Friend through #4 Big Bro. A #.5 Tricam can be placed in the flake on the right, half way up the final section.

67. Right Torpedo Tube 11c A few yards right of the preceding climb is an intimidating arm bar crack above some open air. The first 8 feet are the crux. If you can master that, cruise the rest (just some 11 offwidth). For those with small hands, up the rating a letter grade or two.

68. Gravity's Rainbow 11c A daring undercling leads into *Right Torpedo Tube* about 20 feet up. Climb to this undercling on the right, and grip it all the way to the *Tube.*

69. Grand Traverse 10c Find a small roof around the corner and 10 yards from *Gravity's Rainbow.* Climb a crack line to the right of the roof, going through some blocky shelves, and surmount a bulge to enter a slot (10a). Climb up to the big roof, and traverse right to belay bolts beneath a fist crack. Enter the fist crack (crux), and follow the moderating line to a belay around a chockstone. Rack for Pitch 2: #2.5 through #4 Friends (two of the last). An alternative start, involving rope drag, ascends the dihedral corner at the left side of the small roof and then traverse into the main line. If you rappel after the first pitch, don't say the climb was easy for a 10c.

NORTHWEST SIDE, LEFT END

Fifteen yards right of *Grand Traverse* are two thin curvy cracks, the left one being the lower branch of the second pitch of *Grand Traverse*. Both climbs are elegant and highly recommended. See Fig. 6.9 for an overview of this area.

70. Max Factor 11c Cosmetic elegance for the fingers if not the face. Clamber up some blocks, lean back and get ready for the crux near the bulge. Rappel from bolts at the end of the first pitch of *Grand Traverse,* or climb its second pitch.

71. Bug Squad 11d Once more, climb up some blocks to an exasperatingly difficult lieback near a piton, move past another one, and finish with hard climbing with real gear to belay bolts. Rappel or continue to the top up the now easier crack (a.k.a. *Bandanna Crack*).

72. Baalbek 9 Excellent climb. Site of local deity. Pray that the chockstones don't come out. Six yards right of *Bug Squad* is a deep V shaped groove with some chockstones. Climb the lower part of the groove to a shelf on the left, and tiptoe into the upper part of the groove. Climb past 2 chockstones until forced out of the groove and finish on the finger crack (crux) on the left. Descent options: walk off right, climb an easy chimney and wander down the southeast side; rappel off *Bug Squad* chains.

There are 3 slightly right leaning cracks a few yards right of *Baalbek*: *MaxiLash, Octagon,* and *Vault. Octagon is* a long standing sand bag having been given many spurious ratings starting at 5.9+. As of this writing, it has not received an ascent, although many have tried and even more thought about it. Do the first redpoint ascent, and you'll be enshrined in the Nautilus Hall of Fame.

73. MaxiLash 11a Test piece. As sustained as a desert climb. Scramble up the blocks to the offwidth. Get past the first overhanging section (crux) and up to a constriction. Climb past that and a slightly overhanging section where the crack narrows (lesser crux). Belay on the ledge. Gear: stoppers and #3 Friends to #4 Camalots. Descend as for *Baalbek*.

74. Vault 10a Easier than it looks. Good finger locks and adequate protection. Scramble up the blocks to a small roof. Enter the finger crack above the roof (crux), and continue to an easy chimney. Descent options: climb a chimney on the left to descend from *Middle Parallel Space*; climb a chimney on the right and wander down the southeast face.

THE NAUTILUS
NORTHWEST SIDE
LEFT END

HORTICULTURE ANNEX

69. Grand Traverse 10c   74. Vault 10a
70. Max Factor 11c   75. Captain Nemo 10d
71. Bug Squad 11d   76. Auto Supply H.11b
72. Baalbek 9   79. Horticulture 6
73. Maxilash 11a   80. Cannonball 10a

Figure 6.9

75. Captain Nemo 10d Twelve yards right of *Vault* is a large roof with a right facing dihedral leading to it. Lower down, the dihedral is left facing. Start on the shelves below, and climb to the dihedral which goes from small hands to fists (hardest at the beginning, 5.8). Belay at the chains below the roof. Traverse under the roof (crux) and belay on the shelf on the right. Descent: climb an easy offwidth on the right (last part of *Horticulture)* and wander back to the descent slab for *Hamburger Crack.* The first pitch is a favorite, moderate crack climb.

Horticulture Annex

Horticulture Annex is 35 yards right of *Captain Nemo.* It's infrequently visited because of its northern exposure. However, the listed climbs are all good, and on a warm day the ambiance is agreeable. To descend from the next 4 routes, walk down to the right, or go to the southeast side, turn left and descend as for *Hamburger Crack.* The next two routes are on the left wall (orientation 240°) of the annex.

76. Automotive Supply House 11b This starts on the second crack from the right which is fisty at the start, constricts, then goes to a short, wide slot followed by more fists. Sustained with two distinct cruxes. Some climbers rappel at the slot, but one of the cruxes is climbing out of it. Good climb.

77. In The Groove 10b This easier version of *Automotive* is just right of it. The hard part is an open angle groove which follows a moderate offwidth start. The groove looks like it could be stemmed but is usually climbed with other techniques. Rack: Lots of small stuff and #3 and #4 Friends for the top.

78. Burning Spear 11b Start at *Horticulture,* but after a few feet climb the right facing dihedral that lies between *In the Groove* and *Horticulture.* When the dihedral reaches a roof, move slightly left to join *In the Groove.*

79. Horticulture 6 North side and not too much traffic cause this climb to live up to its name. Nice climb. Do some weeding to help maintain appearances. On the right wall of the annex (oriented at 300°) is a right sloping crack. Climb it to its top, move left (crux), and belay behind a large flake. Climb left behind the flake. Then move into the vertical exit crack.

80. Cannonball 10a Well named since the crux might make you feel like the stunt man at the circus. This route starts 30 yards right of *Horticulture* in a left facing dihedral that changes to right facing and leads to an overhang. Do a 5.3 pitch to the overhang and belay. Pass the overhang using the crack on the left, and continue on the strenuous jams overhead. Medium stoppers and small to medium Friends.

NAUTILUS (NW Side)
The Cool Hand Luke Area

81. Failure to Communicate 10a
82. Cool Hand Luke 10d
83. Devil's Food 9
84. I'm Spartacus 11b

Figure 6.10

Cool Hand Luke Area

A tunnel, formed by a tilted slab and containing a shelf, will be found close to the side of Nautilus and 130 yards right of *Cannonball* . The next climb is 5 yards to the right of the tunnel, and the second one is 15. If approaching from the southwest end of Nautilus, *Cool Hand* is 55 yards left of a big, overhanging, flat roof called the Tongue Depressor. See Fig. 6.10.

81. Failure to Communicate 10a This thin crack system follows bulges and ledges up to a black stained wall above which is a hand crack exiting to a shelf.

82. Cool Hand Luke 10d A more difficult version of *Failure* with a really bulgy crux high up. This interesting route would be climbed more often if the location were less obscure and not north facing.

83. Devil's Food 9 This crack starts at the ground and eventually forms the left juncture of the Tongue Depressor. The crux is the offwidth section near the roof.

84. I'm Spartacus 11b Directly under the Tongue Depressor is a flare with a thin crack in the back of it. Climb the flare until the route ends on a slabby ledge below the roof.

Northwest Side, Right End

The next group of climbs is most easily described by their relationship to the Parabolic Slab and to *Baldwin's Chimney* which splits the Nautilus below the left edge of the Slab (Fig. 6.11). There is a ledge to the left of the Slab and in front of the face below the Slab. There are some overhanging blocks above the ledge. At the left end of this ledge (30 yards left of *Baldwin's Chimney*) is *Old Eyeful*, a route that looks at least 5.11. There used to be rappel bolts to the right of *Humper*. Currently, descent is by scrambling to the left to use the *Escalator* descent, or scrambling to the right to descend as for *Mother #1*.

85. Old Eyeful 7 Climb an easy finger crack to the imposing crack in the ceiling and find the surprising finish. Standard rack through a #3.5 Friend.

Fifteen yards right of *Old Eyeful* is a big slot in the upper blocks. There are cracks on the left and right at the bottom of the slot. The first of these two recommended climbs takes the left crack and the second the right crack which, in its upper part, consists of two cracks separated by a finger of rock.

86. Dual 9- Climb a 5.7 handcrack in a slot to a shelf and belay (30 feet). Get back into the crack on the left (crux) and continue on sustained jamming and

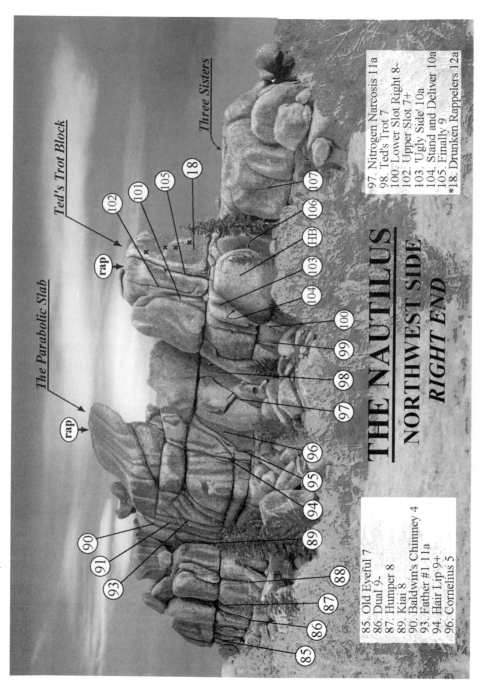

The Parabolic Slab

Ted's Trot Block

Three Sisters

THE NAUTILUS
NORTHWEST SIDE
RIGHT END

85. Old Eyeful 7
86. Dual 9-
87. Humper 8
89. Kiai 8
90. Baldwin's Chimney 4
93. Father #1 11a
94. Hair Lip 9+
96. Cornelius 5

97. Nitrogen Narcosis 11a
98. Ted's Trot 7
100. Lower Slot Right 8-
102. Upper Slot 7+
103. 'Ugly Side' 10a
104. Stand and Deliver 10a
105. Finally 9
*18. Drunken Rappelers 12a

Figure 6.11

stemming to the top. The crux is height dependent (5.9+ for those under 5'4" and 5.7+ for those over 6'3").

87. Humper 8 The American gigolo climb. Third class the easy chimney on the bottom to a shelf where an RP can be placed to protect placing a large Friend which protects getting off the shelf. Offwidth on the left crack until you're able to stem. At this point, the climbing moderates since there are good groin holds. Rack: RP's and #2 through #4 Friends.

There is no really good approach to the next 5 climbs. You can approach from the left or right and do some modestly exposed boulder scaling, or burrow in securely from underneath. In any event, walk towards the climbs along the lower rock bands and then straight up to them. Descent is by downclimbing *Baldwin's Chimney* or rappelling to the southeast from the top of the Parabolic Slab.

88. Hello Stupid 10b According to the first ascensionist, this is a contrived line, but actually it follows natural weaknesses up the wall. Start left of the next route but lower down in an offwidth on the southwest facing wall. At the shelf with a little roof above it, go a little left and follow a thin right leaning crack.

89. Kiai 8 Just left of *Baldwin's Chimney* is a deep slot (facing 220°) with a large finger of rock in it. Climb the crack on the left side of the finger.

90. Baldwin's Chimney 4 This is the sizable chimney at the very left end of the Parabolic Slab. Walk into the chimney until beneath a large chockstone and then climb towards it. Sparse protection.

91. Mother #1 7+ Classic. Just right of the preceding route is a wide groove that eventually narrows to a handcrack. Climbing changes steadily from 5.4 to 5.7. Belay using the chockstones atop *Baldwin's Chimney.*

92. Parabolic Slab Route 2 Start at the top of *Baldwin's Chimney* and angle up right to rappel bolts at the top of the slab, taking the path of least resistance (no protection--years ago bolts were chopped by a fanatic). This route is often climbed just to do the free rappel down the southeast side.

93. Father #1 11a Jack Sprat version of *Mother #1.* A couple of yards right of *Mother* is a handcrack that gradually goes to fingers and then a face exit. The crux is high up. This nice climb does not have much protection near the top beyond an old piton.

94. Hair Lip 9+ This route starts below the right edge of the Parabolic Slab on a wall facing 240°. It is just left of *Easy Jam.* Climb a right leaning crack that leads to two shelves. At the second shelf crawl off to the right (crux). The climb is standard Vedauwoo jamming until the enervating crux which can be done on the back or the belly. Exciting in either case. Save a large Friend for the featured crawl off. Rappelling after the first shelf misses the whole point of the climb.

For descent from the remaining climbs on the Nautilus, see *Route 1*. Also, a quick way to get back to the start of the next two climbs is to use the tunnel that starts right (northeast) of *Bombs Away* and exits to the left (northeast) of *Ted's Trot*. The next two climbs are on the wall below the low spot on the Nautilus contour: right of the Parabolic Slab and left of Ted's Trot Block. A toprope can be set above the wall for face climbing practice.

95. Easy Jam 4 This is the wide crack in the right facing dihedral formed below the right end of the Parabolic Slab. Good practice on offwidth--mostly low fifth 'class with a touch of 5.4 near the top.

96. Cornelius 5 A finger crack angles up right from the start of *Easy Jam* and finishes as a vertical hand crack.

97. Nitrogen Narcosis 11a This curvy crack could give you the bends if you don't get it straight. Fifteen yards left of *Ted's Trot* is a right leaning crack on a wall oriented at 240°. The climb starts as a wide crack, changing to fingers before a double roof, then an overhanging flare to a wide opening, followed by the crux finish when the crack closes down. Get the idea?

98. Ted's Trot 7 Start in the chimney below the left side of Ted Trot's block and climb to a platform and then follow a wide slot to a hand crack. Easy going until the final exit moves. An old time favorite that has been surpassed in recent years by more sustained climbs.

Upper Slot is the conspicuous offwidth towards the right side Ted Trot's Block. Below it and a little to the left, 2 cracks are formed by a finger of rock in a slot. The crack on the left side of the finger is the upper section of *Lower Slot Left* and the crack on the right side is the upper section of *Lower Slot*. For years, *Upper Slot* has been considered the test piece for beginning offwidth climbers and traditionally rated 5.6 (sandbag!). All the *Slot* routes come with high recommendations.

99. Lower Slot Left 7 The crux comes at exiting the route.

100. Lower Slot 8- Entering the upper crack is the crux (a.k.a. as *Lower Slot Right*).

101. Upper Slot Left 10b This begins in the crack just left of *Upper Slot*. Getting started is the whole problem. Eases up to 5.7 after that. **101a. Original Upper Slot Left 7** Avoid the hard part by starting in a left facing dihedral a yard right of the regular start, and traverse back into the route after about 10 feet. There's no protection at the start.

102. Upper Slot 7+ The crux is staying with it during the middle part.

103. A Little On The Ugly Side 10a If there were one more bolt at the beginning, a better name would be in order. This climb is to the left of the next route and starts in an offwidth crack above a hole at the same level as the first shelf of *Lower Slot*. Squiggle up the crack and move left onto a slab. Climb past two old bolts to the *Upper Slot* shelf. The crux is near the second bolt, but a fall at the start, which is difficult to protect, would be serious.

104. Stand and Deliver 10a This route follows three bolts up the scooped out face (orientation 50°) on Harder Boulder (HB), the big boulder to the right of *Lower Slot*. Belay and rappel from bolts on the top. This fun climb receives the Nautilus architecture award for the best placed set of bolts at Vedauwoo. The crux start is well protected by the first bolt. It's a little runout between the second and third bolts, but the climbing is easier there.

105. Finally 9 Recommended. A test piece for the aspiring offwidth climber. This offwidth crack is just around the corner to the right from *Upper Slot*. Start in a right facing dihedral. Climb the crack to a small roof, pass it on the right, and then more or less face climb to the top and a finger crack exit.

106. Harder Than Your Husband 12c This intimidating, overhanging finger crack is in an alley on the southwest side of Harder Boulder. Many wives have toproped it after climbing *Stand and Deliver*.

107. Par Four 8 This route is 10 yards to the right of the right end of Harder Boulder. It faces 300° and is part of a crack system forming a figure 4. Ascend the branching part of the 4.

7. POLAND HILL

Poland Hill is the first major formation visible on the left after taking the Vedauwoo cutoff (see Fig. 1.3). It is easily identified by its rat brain shape with *Fantasia* forming the longitudinal fissure between the rocky hemispheres. Poland Hill is actually a complex of several distinct crags harboring many classical and amusing climbs. You can approach the area by turning left onto the dirt road just past the entrance, bearing right, driving as far as feasible, and then hiking the rest of the way. A more scenic approach hikes into Holy Saturday. When you are about half way to Holy Saturday, you can see Poland Hill straight to the west (left). Go about 100 yards past Holy Saturday, cross over on the first beaver dam, and, heading southwest, aim towards Poland Hill. Principal orienting features are *Overload, Skull,* and *Fantasia*. The routes will be described counterclockwise starting at the southeast end of the complex. Descents can be fashioned by down climbing towards the south or west. *Routes (9-20)* use the rappel bolts at the top of *Route 11*. The wall containing *Routes 1-6* faces 140°. See Fig. 7.1 for these climbs.

> *Skull*--a classic.
> **Jam, lieback,
> stem up the start
> .. puzzle thru the
> beginning of the
> 2nd pitch...**

SOUTHEAST SIDE

1.   Overload 9 Start at a right leaning hand crack, and then move left into a small, cave like structure. Medium to large Friends and a few medium stoppers. Too much gear will overload you on the penultimate move (crux).

2.   Rocking Chair 10d Eight yards right of *Overload* is a flaky, funky crack system formed by pages. The crack system faces 60°. Ascend this to a roof. Step left, and pull over the roof at a crack (crux). Walk forward a few feet, ascend (10a) a short steep headwall with a crack at its top, and belay. Except for the cruxes the climbing on this interesting route is moderate.

3.   Under Achiever 7 Start 10 yards right of *Rocking Chair* in an offwidth running in the same direction as the *Rocking Chair* crack system. Ascend this to a deep recess, and then climb to the top using the nice hand crack on the right.

4.   Orbital Ridge 10b This route starts 33 yards right of *Overload* on the overhanging, left side of a dihedral corner oriented at 40°. The wall on which it occurs is at the left end of a large alcove. Don't be browbeaten by this arching crack. Good jamming all the way with a crux exit. Rappel descent.

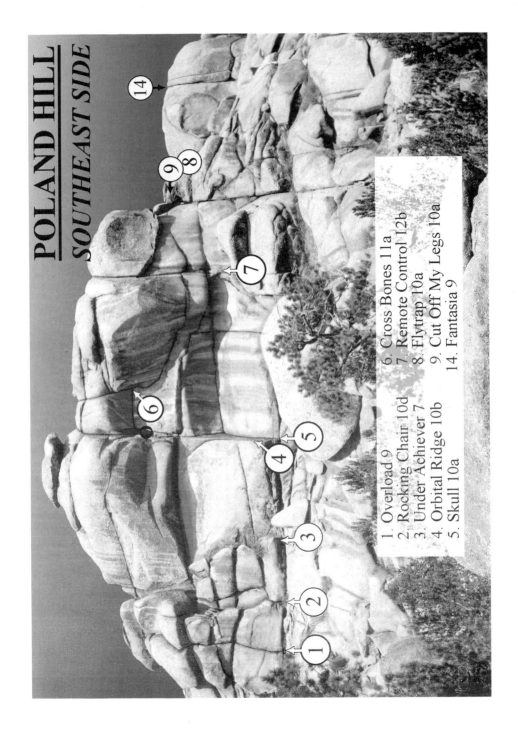

POLAND HILL
SOUTHEAST SIDE

1. Overload 9
2. Rocking Chair 10d
3. Under Achiever 7
4. Orbital Ridge 10b
5. Skull 10a
6. Cross Bones 11a
7. Remote Control 12b
8. Flytrap 10a
9. Cut Off My Legs 10a
14. Fantasia 9

Figure 7.1

Figure 7.2 Steve Seckinger styling on *Kim* (5.6).

5. Skull 10a Classic. Use your head on this climb, or else you could become an anatomy specimen. The route starts just right of *Orbital Ridge*. From the belay on a platform, move up about 20 feet to the start of an overhanging hand crack in a dihedral corner. Lieback, jam, and stem your way up the next 20 feet (crux), and continue another 25 feet until a convenient belay can be set up. Puzzle through the early crux on pitch 2 which continues straight up through a small roof.

6. Cross Bones 11a This alternate exit traverses under the roof (right) from the belay at the end of *Skull*'s first pitch and then follows a rising crack for about 10 feet (crux) to a little ledge. Continue up the crack straight above. Protection: RP's through #2 Friends.

7. Remote Control 12b This climb is a few yards to the right of the alcove containing *Skull*. It ascends a crack in a right facing dihedral to a little ceiling formed by a slanting overhang on the right. The thin, tricky start (TCU's) leads to a 5.11 handcrack. Very sustained and very recommended.

The next two routes are 50 yards right of *Remote Control on* a wall facing 80°. See Fig. 7.1.

8. Flytrap 10a Zipper up for this one, or you could get hung up. Climb a thin crack for about 40 feet. Jog left a foot and a half at a very small ledge, and ascend an offwidth that narrows to a hand crack after 15 feet. Double set of RP's for the thin section. The name refers to an incident on the first ascent.

9. Cut Off My Legs and Call Me Shorty 10a The most prominent feature of this climb, which is about 5 yards right of *Flytrap*, is a small roof with a handcrack above it. Squiggle up to the roof, most conveniently done from the right side, and jam away. This route is better than the song for which it was named.

THE RAT BRAIN

Fantasia is 150 yards to the right (N) of *Remote Control.* Before getting to the *Fantasia Wall*, you can go left through some boulders to get to the southwest side of the crag on which the following three climbs are found.

10. Little Old Crack 5 The name says it all. A 30 foot hand crack splits the left end of the face.

11. Southwest Friction 4 A pleasant route that goes past two bolts on the face.

12. Kim 6 Follow the arching handcrack on the right side of the wall to the top. Superb.

POLAND HILL

RAT BRAIN

FANTASIA WALL

11. Southwest Friction 4
12. Kim 6
13. Piece of Dirt 11a
14. Fantasia 9
15. Cool Jet 11c
16. Petit Crapon 9

Big Flake

rap

Figure 7.3

The next four routes are on the Fantasia Wall (140°). See Fig. 7.3

13. Piece of Dirt 11a Once aptly named, this is now a fine climb after the first ascensionist added some bolts. The route starts just left of *Fantasia* in a thin line masquerading as a crack. Continue up the face following the bolts.

14. Fantasia 9 Classic. The great longitudinal fissure. The crux is getting into the crack. This was rated 5.10 in 1970 and the hardest climb at Vedauwoo. Then the locals became expert at offwidths and changed the rating.

15. Cool Jet 11c The start is the crux on this thin crack which lies just to the right of *Fantasia*.

16. Petit Crapon 9 The fissure of Sylvius. Start in an offwidth in an alcove on the right end of the face. After reaching a platform, go left and finish with some delicate face moves using the "super undercling" (crux).

THE RAT BRAIN, EAST WALL

The next two climbs are on the east side (80°) around the corner from *Petit Crapon*. *Sugar Crack* is the first climbable crack encountered. See Fig. 7.4

17. Sugar Crack 7- Sweet stemming on a sunny autumn morning. Climb a groove which has its crux at the exit. Belay on a ledge. Move forward and climb the right side of the face, eventually moving right (north) around a corner before proceeding to the top.

18. Tanfasia 9+ Unique. Begin 3 yards to the right of *Sugar Crack*. The rock at the start is friable so be careful in setting protection (extra #3.5 and #4 Friends). Climb up to a fist jam, and follow it to a sloping shelf. Go left on the spectacular 5.9 crawl off (#3.5 Friend).

19. Boulder Hop 9+ Continue walking to the right for about 30 yards from *Tanfasia* until you arrive at a small alcove in a wall facing 340°. The route ascends the crack in the recess of the alcove. The traditional rating for this climb is 5.6. (There is a 6 move--when you sit down for the belay.)

20. Bolder Hopper 9 After the first pitch of *Sugar Crack,* walk 13 yards forward into the hallway, and find a handcrack in the left wall. Ascend by stemming until a bold hop is required to enter the crack. Taller climbers will find this easier since they can make the bold hop higher on the route. *Boulder Hop* is a preferred first pitch--more consistent to the route in rating and name. You can also get to this climb by going to the middle of the north side of the wall and traversing back to the climb along a shelf (a.k.a. *Ape Walk*).

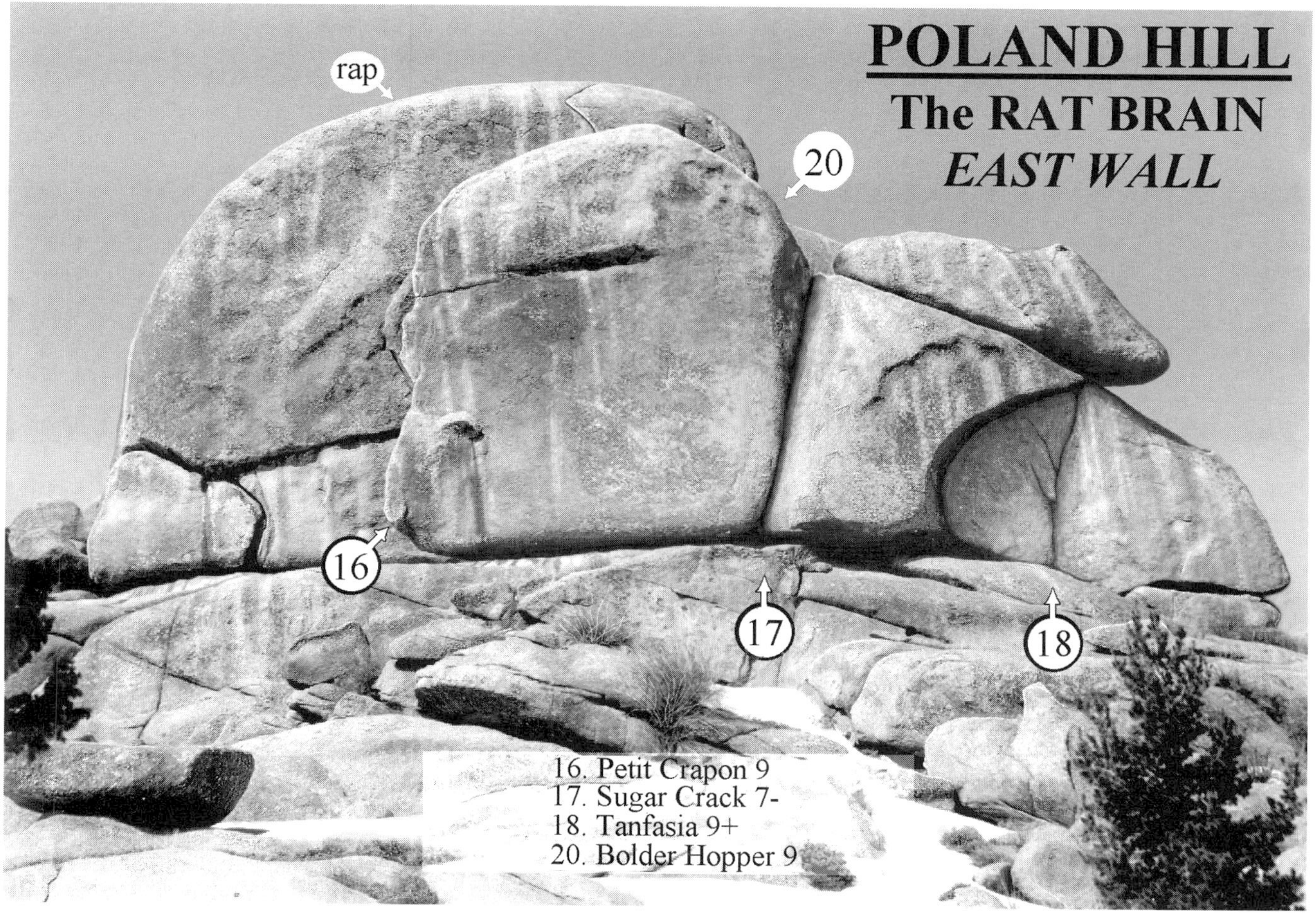

POLAND HILL
The RAT BRAIN
EAST WALL

16. Petit Crapon 9
17. Sugar Crack 7-
18. Tanfasia 9+
20. Bolder Hopper 9

Figure 7.4

About 75 yards west (right) of *Boulder Hop* is a southwest facing alcove with two left leaning cracks on the right wall (320°). Just before getting there, the following climb can be found on a wall facing 240°.

21. Coming Up Short 9 A 25 foot offwidth with one hard move at the top.

22. Clean and Jerk 9- There is a large, prominent flake left of the two cracks. Climb the hand crack on the left side of the flake.

23. Clean and Press 9 Climb the right side of the flake which, after a few hard moves, opens into an easy chimney formed by the flake and the wall.

24. Stem Christy 8- Climb the two left leaning cracks. The rating is 5.6 A1 if ski poles are used.

8. VALLEY MASSIF

Valley Massif is a little over a mile from the Central Area. Surrounded by beaver ponds and aspen groves, it is one of the loveliest places in Vedauwoo, especially in the autumn when the approach is driest and the aspen is in color. It can be reached in three ways. Walk past the Holy Saturday cliff (on your right) and proceed north about another quarter mile. Valley Massif will be the prominent crag on the left across the beaver ponds. Walk across the first suitable beaver dam. Occasionally, this is wet going. Due to this surrounding moisture, Valley Massif is one of the few areas at Vedauwoo where insect repellent can come in handy. A more alpine approach starts at the end of the Robber's Roost Road.

> **Screw 5.7 Outstanding jamming ... must for any aspiring crack climber**

From thence, hike west up the old nature trail at the end of the road heading for the gap between the two high points, and then scramble down to the beaver ponds. The third approach is by way of Reynolds Hill. Instead of making the final turn right to get to Reynold's, continue on a short way, then turn right going 0.7 mile until the road ends at a buck board fence. Cross the fence, then the stream, and pick up a trail heading west.

NORTHWEST SIDE

The northwest side of Valley Massif has a splendid collection of moderate, mostly two pitch, crack climbs as well as a few very hard new routes. Descent is by walk down to the northeast end of the rock or by rappel bolts on the wall to the right and just below the top of *Hammer*. The best spot for an overall view is atop the hill northwest of Valley Massif from whence the principal orienting features are clearly visible (see Fig. 8.1). A sizable block at the right (southwest) end of the summit platform forms the high point of the crag. Two vertical cracks lie below the left and right ends of the block. The one on the left is the last pitch of *Zipper*. The one on the right is *Hammer*. The 3 parallel cracks below and in front of the start of the last pitch of *Zipper* are *Button, Snap,* and the 2nd pitch of *Zipper*. To the left of *Button* is *Monkey Wrench*, and, a little to the left of it is *Screw*.

1. Soft Touch 5 This can be done in 2 or 3 pitches. An easy fist crack leads to a large boulder on the first ledge--a good place to belay to minimize rope drag. The crux (perhaps a move of 6 or 7) climbs out from the boulder. Continue up a slot belaying near its top. Pass a roof on the right, and ascend a chimney to the top. This is an interesting and exciting climb--one of the best at its grade.

The next two climbs start 23 yards right of *Soft Touch* in a wide low angle crack.

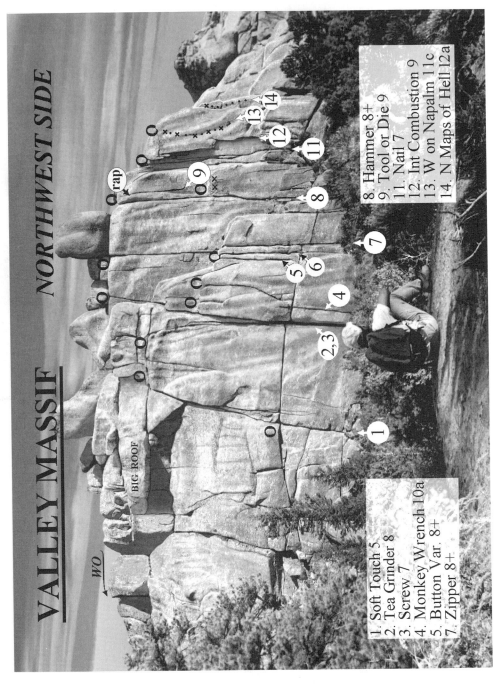

Figure 8.1

2. Tea Grinder 8 A mellow brew with a little kick at the end. First pitch is a full rope length. Climb the common start to *Tea Grinder* and *Screw* , but bear left and climb a short, strenuous chimney. Pass its roof on the left, and continue on a crack for 50 feet. Belay below the crux--a short pitch of offwidth.

3. Screw 7 Outstanding jamming and a must for any aspiring crack climber. It don't get no better even if the reference is to hardware and not physiology. Bear right where *Tea Grinder* goes left following a handcrack to a platform. Belay there to minimize rope drag. Climb a short, almost horizontal pitch, to another platform below a head wall. The last pitch ascends a perfect 5.6 handcrack that leaves you with a great feeling at the finish.

4. Monkey Wrench 10a This starts just right of *Screw* and would be a great climb if the crux could be better protected. Climb a moderate offwidth to a ledge about 30 feet off the deck. Then ascend a right leaning crack that is difficult to protect at its beginning. Don't monkey around there. Once past this spot the climbing eases up and shares the last pitch of *Screw*.

Thirteen yards left of Hammer are 3 lines forming a parallel circuit with a common start and a common exit. The next 3 routes ascend the various lines in the circuit.

5. Button Variation 8+ Start at the end of the first pitch of *Zipper.* Traverse left to the leftmost of the 3 parallel cracks. Climb the sustained hand crack which is difficult to protect because the crack is bottomed out and collects dirt.

6. Snap Variation 8 This is the middle crack. Move slightly left from the belay at the end of the first pitch of *Zipper* to a slot. Enter the slot, and continue up a crack that becomes gradually smaller.

7. Zipper 8+ Begin in the stiff 8+ offwidth that forms the common start to the parallel circuit. After 40 feet belay on a small ledge. Continue straight up on moderate, but wild, 5.8 climbing, and belay on a platform. The last pitch is a truly splendid 7+ handcrack.

The next 2 routes are most easily identified by the inverted V slot above a ledge half way up the wall. The slot forms the beginning of *Tool or Die.*

8. Hammer 8+ Climb an easy wide crack that leads to a spacious belay ledge with bolts. Finish on a sustained offwidth that starts on the left end of the ledge.

9. Tool or Die 9 Same first pitch as *Hammer.* Ascend the inverted V slot to a handcrack. The first moves are the crux and are easier for the tall or flexible.

10. SB 11d There is a thin seam just right of *Tool or Die*. Climb the seam, and follow the bolts to the top after the seam fades. A demanding route that requires good skill in placing protection.

A prominent apse is situated near the right end of the wall and some 10 yards right of *Hammer*. It's formed by a recess in the main wall and a huge flake on the right end of the wall. Descent for all the remaining routes on the northwest side is by scrambling to the south and descending as for *Ladder*.

11. Nail 7 The name is allegorical and not an invitation to use pitons. A mellow climb for a lazy summer afternoon as you ascend the cracks in the rear of the apse.

12. Internal Combustion 9 Carefully deciding which side of your body will be internal to the rock will keep you from overheating. At the right side of the apse, a crack in a left facing dihedral leads to an overhang which is passed on the left and then up a wide crack to the top.

13. Whaling on Napalm 11c Begin close to the start of *Internal Combustion* and traverse right onto the flake. Follow a line of bolts that leads up the depression in the middle of the face.

14. New Maps of Hell 12b This starts in a cavernous crack on the right side of the flake. Scramble up to the crack prepared for sustained striving. There is one bolt and the crack takes big gear, nonetheless there is real potential for a long fall. A true test piece for muscle and nerve.

SOUTHEAST SIDE

The southeast side of Valley Massif is not as heavily trafficked as the northwest side, but early in the morning there's no better place to warm up cold muscles. Descent from all the routes can be achieved by walkoff to the northeast. This can be a bit involved, but persist in taking the line of least resistance. An alternate descent path, most useful for the first 3 routes below, is to traverse right a few yards, then scramble through a hallway to the northwest side, and rappel from the top of *Hammer*.

At the right end of the cliff is a hallway formed by a big flagstone in front of the main wall. *Powder Puff* starts in the left end of the hallway (see Fig. 8.2). A second orienting feature is *Hooker* in the middle of the wall. This ascends a prominent left facing dihedral which ends in a roof going to the left. Two parallel cracks, about 15 feet, apart arise from a thick aspen grove at the left end of the wall . The left one ascends the entire wall, and the right one stops about two thirds the way

VALLEY MASSIF
SOUTHEAST SIDE

16. S S Ran Out 8
19. Dreaming of Babylon 10c
21. Quits 9+
21. Falcon's Lair 7
22. Hollerith Exit 8
23. Bill Steal 6

24. Klarren 7
25. Hooker 10c
26. Sunny Day 5
27. Cyber-Way 11a
28. Bittersweet 9
29. Powder Puff 5

Figure 8.2

up after passing a small arching headwall that is to its right. A third and less prominent crack is right of these two cracks.

15. Ladder 7+ Start in the third crack, and after about 10 feet follow the line of least resistance as you traverse left into the first crack. Follow the first crack up to the final headwall and belay (2 pitches of 5.3). Finish on the wide crack above which contains an isolated move of 5.8. Beware of escaping right on easier rock since that way lacks protection.

16. Social Security Ran Out 8 This is easy going at first, but the protection is not so good as you age on the route. Again start in the third crack, but remain in it until the crack gradually fades into obscurity. Then move up unprotected to the little arching headwall (big gear) described above. Belay near right end of the headwall (130 feet and 5.4). Find a little crack that is about 20 feet above the headwall and to its left. Climb unprotected face to the crack, and continue straight up to the crux offwidth exit (80 feet and 5.8).

17. Reverse ? Mark 7 Start as in the preceding route, but after the first pitch angle up right for 70 feet on unprotected face (a.k.a. *Social Security)*.

18. East Face 4 This is a strange name for a chimney that does not face east. There is a group of huge blocks atop the left (southwest) side of Valley Massif. This climb ascends a chimney on the right side of the leftmost block.

19. Dreaming of Babylon 10c Twenty yards left of *Quits* is a left facing lieback flake leading to a finger crack. The obvious, exciting crux is entering the finger crack.

Warning: **Do not climb the next 3 routes before July 15 because of nesting raptors.**

20. Quits 9+ This interesting and varied climb starts 33 yards left of *Hooker.* Climb an easy trough to an overhanging finger crack. Lieback and jam past it, and belay on a shelf (8+). Continue up the crack until you arrive at the big platform that runs along the top of Valley Massif, and belay there. A huge flake is at the back of the ledge, and a big block is to its right. The top of the block is the high point of the crag. Climb a left sloping crack that lies between the flake and the block (9+). Consider *Hollerith Exit* as an alternative to the third pitch.

21. Falcon's Lair 7 Instead of climbing the finger crack in *Quits,* sneak right and follow a line of cracks to the big ledge. Descend or climb the next route.

22. Hollerith Exit 8 Ascend the hand/fist crack on the right side of the block mentioned in describing the 3rd pitch of *Quits.*

23. Bill Steal 6   A few yards left of *Hooker* is a crack in a small right facing dihedral. Since it tends to get vegetated, everybody benefits if you garden this fine route.

24. Klarren 7   This route starts in an apse past a jumble of boulders 25 yards to the north of the finishes of *Bill Steal* and *Sunny Day*. Jam one of the cracks on either side of the apse until it is possible to stem at which point the climbing eases up.

25. Hooker 10c   A left facing dihedral with a thin seam that suddenly enlarges half way up. At its top a stimulating traverse under the roof hooks up with *Bill Steal*. The rating takes into account the effort needed to protect the first 15 feet.

26. Sunny Day 5   A prominent right facing dihedral starts about 20 feet above the ground and some 20 yards left of the hallway at the right end of the crag. Jam or lieback the dihedral to the ledge above it.

27. Cyber-Way 11a   Sixteen yards right of *Sunny Day* is a thin ramp slanting right. Follow the line suggested by this ramp past two bolts and up to a ledge with the crux after the second bolt.

28. Bittersweet 9   If the old chopped bolt has not been replaced, this could be bitter but not sweet. Climb the easy chimney formed by the flagstone at the right end of the wall, and traverse left past the bolt (crux) to a vertical crack.

29. Powder Puff 4 and Corbel Exit 5   Start as for *Bittersweet,* but continue straight up to an excellent handcrack leading to a ledge. Exit right, or, better yet, step left and mantle on a corbel of rock (5.5 and unprotected) and finish on a friction slab.

9. REYNOLD'S COMPLEX

R|eynold's Hill and the area vaguely to the north of it have been known at various times as Grand Vedauwoo or Devil's Playground. The name *Grand Vedauwoo* fell into disuse decades ago. Reynold's Hill became intensely developed in the 1970's and emerged as the predominant crag in this area of Vedauwoo. As a result, its name became associated with the entire section. At that point, the name *Devil's Playground* developed a more narrow usage associated with a specific crag to the east of Reynold's Hill. Other terms, such as the inelegant *Behind Reynold's Hill,* were used to describe the area adjacent to Reynold's Hill proper. For the entire area, we use the term *Reynold's Complex* which, while lacking the cachet of Devil's Playground, conveys well the complicated nature of this intriguing area of splendid climbing.

The Southwest Face of Reynold's Hill contains the most dense collection of climbs in the 6-11 range at Vedauwoo. Most are crack climbs though many contain a face component. There are fewer climbs on the East Face, but these include some moderate classics, e.g., *Moor Crossing* and *Tombstone Crack,* and on cold mornings it warms up early.

At 2.4 miles past the Central Area Turnoff, the east side of Reynold's Hill comes into view at 11:00 with the magnificent soaring dihedral of *Coffee Grinder* visible at the southeast end (if approaching from Happy Jack Road, it's 4.9 miles to the Reynold's Hill turnoff). Immediately after that, turn left on 700D for .7 mile bearing right on 700DC at the first real fork in the road. Park shortly after that. Cross the stream left of where a spring gushes from an irrigation pipe and follow a path to the right (north) to the crag, crossing another stream along the way. (Climbers often drive another .2 mile to the end of the road, but it's more difficult to ford the stream there.) As you get near Reynold's Hill, an old jeep road goes up towards its southeast end. To get to climbs that are on the Southwest Face and left of *Like Fun,* turn left about 70 yards before reaching the southeast end of the crag. Then just hike towards your chosen climb. For routes on the southwest face right of *Like Fun,* continue on the road until near the southeast tip of the formation. Scramble up a ramp and slot to gain the ledge below *Guide Book Dilemma.* For climbs on the East Face, continue on the jeep road and scramble up to the cliff near the base of *Moor Crossing* or *Horror Show.* Now hike up the gully at the base of the cliff to get to other climbs on the East Face.

> ...an extraordinary apse containing 3 superb crack climbs. *Climb and Punishment 5.9+* has 70 feet of solid hand jams..

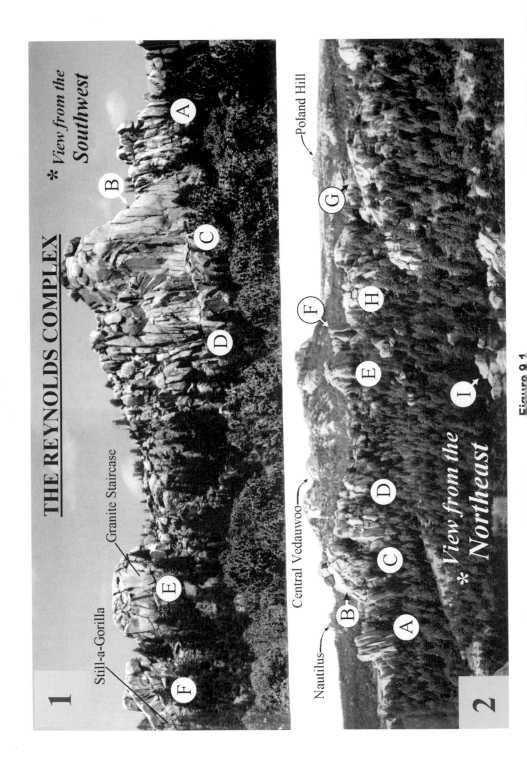

THE REYNOLDS COMPLEX

View from the Southwest

Still-a-Gorilla

Granite Staircase

Nautilus

Central Vedauwoo

Poland Hill

View from the Northeast

Figure 9.1

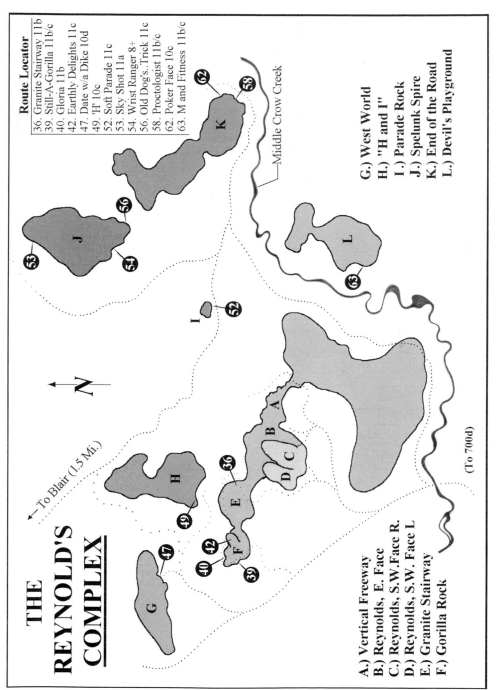

THE
REYNOLD'S
COMPLEX

Route Locator

36. Granite Stairway 11b
39. Still-A-Gorilla 11b/c
40. Gloria 11b
42. Earthly Delights 11c
47. Date w/a Dike 10d
49. 'H' 10c
52. Soft Parade 11c
53. Sky Shot 11a
54. Wrist Ranger 8+
56. Old Dog's. Trick 11c
58. Proctologist 11b/c
62. Poker Face 10c
63. M and Fitness 11b/c

A.) Vertical Freeway
B.) Reynolds, E. Face
C.) Reynolds, S.W.Face R.
D.) Reynolds, S.W. Face L
E.) Granite Stairway
F.) Gorilla Rock

G.) West World
H.) "H and I"
I.) Parade Rock
J.) Spelunk Spire
K.) End of the Road
L.) Devil's Playground

← To Blair (1.5 Mi.)

Middle Crow Creek

(To 700d)

Figure 9.2

East Face of Reynold's Hill

The descriptions of the East Face routes differ a little from some of the earliest accounts: lines have been rationalized and don't follow all the meanderings that once characterized them. Orientation routes are *Barf Bucket Traverse* and *Tombstone Crack*. Descent: in general walk far right (north) from the top and downclimb the East Face. Avoid going too far south as you downclimb. See Fig. 9.3.

1. Moor Crossing 6 One of the best at its grade--from chimney to airy face. The route starts 26 yards from the left end of the wall and in front of a huge pine tree. Begin in a trough facing 140°. After 50 feet go straight up through a tight chimney and squeeze through an embrasure formed by chockstones. This pitch protects well and has a few isolated moves of 5.7. An easier alternative for the last section of this pitch is to climb a little to the right in a hard to protect trough. Belay on a spacious platform to the right. Follow along the huge flake on the left wall climbing past an obvious protuberance extending onto the wall, and belay there. The next pitch traverses right for about 25 feet (unprotected) and then surmounts a small head wall near a crack (crux). Climb the face above (unprotected) until you can enter the *Horror Show* chimney on the right. Belay from a cranny on the right near the top of the chimney. Descent: walk right (north) through a hallway and downclimb an easy chimney. Continue north until joining up with the standard descent.

2. Nexus 6 Use the same start as preceding route, but after 40 feet traverse right under a huge shield like flake and belay at the *Horror Show* chimney. Continue slanting up right on the face until about the middle of the roof on *Barf Bucket Traverse,* and continue on that climb.

3. Horror Show 9 This was once considered a study in insecurity, but it now protects nicely with a #4 Friend and a #4 Camalot. The route starts 7 yards right of *Moor Crossing* in a chimney facing 90°. The first pitch of 5.2 goes up the crack to a belay below a roof. Pass the roof on the left (crux) using the obvious offwidth crack which gradually becomes smaller and the climbing easier. Near the top, belay in a cranny on the right side of the chimney.

4. Original Horror Show 9 The original route did not ascend the offwidth crux but climbed the equally difficult but now unprotected face on the left (scene of ancient bolt wars).

5. Barf Bucket Traverse 6 This is a pleasant outing whose appearance and exposure are more impressive than the technical difficulties. Start at the belay at the end of the first pitch of *Horror Show.* Traverse right, underneath the roof, all way to the exit chimney on *Tombstone Crack.*

Figure 9.3

Figure 9.4   Climbers on the third pitch of Moor Crossing (5.6).

6. Tombstone Crack 8 Scramble up the gully from *Horror Show,* cross a huge dead tree and 17 yards further another dead tree. The climb starts 10 yards past there in a thin, 12 foot, right leaning crack (small wires) in an open book that leads to a groove. Follow the groove to its end, and belay below a roof. Climb up a short finger crack under the roof (8), move out left onto the face. Finish in a 20 foot chimney which has a crack in its back wall that takes small gear. This fun route requires a variety of techniques.

SOUTHWEST FACE OF REYNOLD'S HILL, LEFT SIDE

The principal orienting features on this face are: *Pooh Corner* which is at the left end of the face; a projecting pile of boulders just right of *K.P.; Glenda's Chimney* which is in the middle of the face and directly beneath the low spot of the profile of the face; the rectangular apse harboring *Climb and Punishment; Coffee Grinder--* the big dihedral corner at the right end. A little to the right of the projecting pile is a descent gully used to get from the climbs right of *Like Fun* to those left of it. Descent from all climbs from *Pooh Corner* through *Hung Like A Horse* is by scrambling back to the enclosed valley behind *Glenda's Chimney* and rappelling that route. Getting there from climbs left of *Labyrinth* involves route finding and non-trivial downclimbing. See Figs. 9.5 and 9.6.

A right facing dihedral corner (left wall faces 110°) at the far left end of the cliff harbors a 50 foot hand crack which widens and pierces a big slanting roof. This is *Pooh Corner.*

7. Pooh Corner 10b Climb the handcrack to the shelf on the left below the roof (9), and master the crux offwidth slot above. Many climbers rappel from the bolts at the shelf thus enjoying the delicious appetizer but not the main course. The climb is easily done as one pitch, but a belay is often set up on the shelf. Besides using *Glenda's Chimney,* one can descend by scrambling to the left.

8. Howling 11a At the shelf on *Pooh Corner,* traverse right 8 feet and take the thin crack through the roof. This variation is a howler since it has almost no protection.

9. Black Starr Chimney 6 Twenty four yards right of *Pooh Corner* is a big chimney (facing 160°) formed by flat flaring walls. The route is easier than it looks.

10. Serpentine 9+ The second pitch is classic. Begin two yards right of the preceding route in a left facing dihedral leading to an offwidth slot. Follow the slot (9) to a platform and belay. Continue straight up the sustained fist\offwidth crack threatening above. Pitch 2 is a.k.a. *Roberts' Rectification* or *R.R.* .

Figure 9.5

REYNOLD'S HILL
Southwest Face, Left Side

Figure 9.6

11. Hesitation 8 Two yards right of *Serpentine* is a wide slot that continues through some pages as it eventually reaches the *Serpentine* belay (6). Start as for the second pitch of *Serpentine,* but early on veer right on a ramp and belay below a left facing dihedral. Climb the dihedral crack (8).

12. Rag--Tag 8+ An alternate second pitch for *Hesitation.* There is a distinctive, left facing dihedral a few yards right of the end of the first pitch of *Hesitation.* Climb the handcrack in the dihedral, and belay in a niche below a huge chockstone.

13. Vacillation Exit 9+ From the belay at the end of *Rag--Tag*, climb out the right side of the chockstone and up a slot to a small shelf. Finish on a crack in a right facing, bulging dihedral (crux).

A notable left facing dihedral is to the right of *Hesitation.* The dihedral's right face, formed by a jutting flange, looks due west. *K.P.,* a left leaning, undulating, wide crack is on this face.

14. K.P. 9- Scramble up some ramps, and literally slither your way to the top of the crack. Finish with some face moves to reach the belay ledge (a.k.a. *Kopow*).

15. Klink 10a A thin crack leading to the start of *K.P.* is on the right end of the flange. Climb the crack and belay. Pitch 2 ascends the 10a hand crack to the right of *K.P.* When the crack intersects a south facing friction ramp, turn left and finish on the ramp (unprotected 9).

16. Maiden 6 This route starts somewhat lower, around the corner, and 6 yards right of *Hesitation.* Climb a pleasant looking handcrack (oriented at 200°).

17. Matron 8 Just right of *Maiden,* a broad crack lies between a huge boulder and the main wall. Ascend this more mature and difficult version of *Maiden.*

SOUTHWEST FACE OF REYNOLD'S HILL, RIGHT SIDE

A jumble of boulders projects out from the cliff some 15 yards right of *Matron.* The next group of climbs is situated to the right of this obstacle on a shelf that starts at *Like Fun. See* Figs. 9.7 and 9.8 for climbs past *Labyrinth.*

18. Like Fun 6 Begin 7 yards left of the transition gully on the right side of the flange containing *K.P.* Climb a chockstone filled chimney exiting to the left.

19. More Fun 6 Start as in the preceding climb but move right and exit in a wide groove.

20. Cosmic Debris 8+ We are but the dust of burnt out stars. Directly above the transition gully is a slot leading to a fine handcrack. Thinking man's climb: always face the correct way.

21. Labyrinth 9 There is an apse just right of the transition gully. A startlingly unique, triangular chimney is found on the left side of the apse. Climb the chimney to a shelf, and belay (8). Move right a little and climb a partially opened book to the top.

22. Connecticut Yankee 10c A slot leading to a handcrack leading to a niche is found on the right side of the apse. Climb to the niche (9), and move slightly left into another handcrack for 10 feet of hard climbing.

23. Glenda's Chimney 5 This obvious and important orienting feature, a deep left slanting groove, is positioned in the middle of the face Currently, it is used more often as a descent path than as a climb.

24. Fat Man's Demise 7 Start in *Glenda's Chimney*. After a few feet move right into a wide crack, and follow it all the way up exiting on the left side of the finger at the top of *Finger Grinder*.

25. Finger Grinder 9 This fine climb sure beats an organ grinder like *Humper*. Start just right of Glenda's Chimney in a right leaning slot with a flake on its left side. Aim for the finger of rock above, and finish on its right side.

A fantastic apse, housing 3 superb crack climbs, sits to the right of *Glenda's Chimney*. Each route involves very sustained jamming and has a distinctive crux. Descent is via *Glenda's Chimney* although from time to time rappel slings have appeared--a practice not to be encouraged.

26. Climb and Punishment 9+ Getting off the ground is the crux (maybe 10a). It's followed by 70 feet of sustained hand jams. At the end of the crack, set up a belay beside a large spike of rock on the right. The fun second pitches leads out left via a cleft to a shelf (50 feet and 5.8). After completing the first ascent in 1871, Feodor Dostoyevsky exclaimed, "Climb ethically, or be sentenced to read *Brothers Karamazov* in the outhouse!"

27. Penis Dimension 10c Consistently more difficult than the preceding route, this climb has a difficult move at the end where the crack widens. Belay shortly after the crux.

28. Hung Like A Horse 11a Repeat the preceding description.

29. Climbs of Passion Exit 11c Climb the first 50 feet of *Climb and Punishment*, and exit by way of a finger crack on the left wall.

Figure 9.7

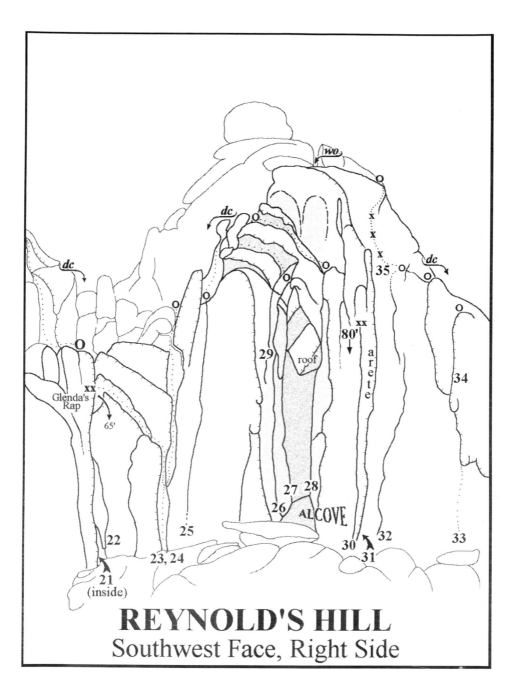

REYNOLD'S HILL
Southwest Face, Right Side

Figure 9.8

30. I'd Rather Be in Philadelphia 12a Classic. If it's not New York, it's all Hoboken. An obvious hand to finger crack facing 150° starts 3 yards left of *Coffee Grinder*. It's hard all the way but gets more difficult as the crack thins higher up. Rappel (80 feet).

31. Coffee Grinder 9 This is most visual line at Vedauwoo -- a long, rising, arching crack that spans the whole southwest side of Reynold's Hill. Enter a big opening lined with pages. Climb to the top of the pages and grapple with a narrower section. Then push through a chimney to a small headwall with a handcrack on the right. Climb the handcrack (#3.5 Friend) and belay on a shelf (5.9, 150 feet). Pitch 2 is an easy 50 feet to the *Horror Show* belay.

There are two ways to finish the next 3 climbs: go straight ahead (north) to join *Moor Crossing*; climb *Ain't Crack Headwall.* Use the East Face descent in both cases.

32. Ain't Crack 8 Begin in a right leaning groove in the right side of the recess in which *Coffee Grinder* originates. When the groove fades away, make an exciting face traverse right to join the *Guide Book Dilemma* crack.

33. Guide Book Dilemma 9 Seventeen yards right of *Coffee Grinder* is a roof that overhangs some 10 feet and resembles elephant's feet. Climb the dihedral just left of the roof, traverse left using a wide undercling, and follow another left facing dihedral for 20 feet. As the dihedral starts to bend right, go left along a flake to a crack and follow it to a belay stance on a platform.

34. Whirligig Exit 8+ In the preceding route, go right instead of left as the dihedral bends right.

35. Ain't Crack Headwall 9 From the belay at the top of *Ain't Crack,* go left to follow a line of 3 bolts up the headwall on sharp, pointy rock. Slant right after the last bolt.

GRANITE STAIRCASE AND GORILLA ROCK

The next two crags can be seen by looking left while standing near the left end of the Southwest Face of Reynold's Hill. The first of these crags, Granite Staircase, has an obvious, flat, face oriented to the southwest. Scramble across a gully to the northwest of Reynold's Hill aiming for this face. As you get near it, contour to the right until you get to a northwest facing wall. The next climb is at the right end of this wall. See Fig. 9.1.

36. Granite Stairway 11b Ascend the line of three bolts up a water streak to the upper floor. There is a rappel station near the top of the route. The first bolt is

Figure 9.9 Granite Staircase, North Face.

fairly far off the deck so be careful not to fall down the stairs.

The next two climbs are approximately 150 yards further to the right going counterclockwise around Granite Staircase. They are found on a wall facing 340°. See Fig. 9.9. Use the *Granite Stairway* descent.

37. Top Flight 8 Climb to a ledge, and then follow the crack to the top where it ends up beneath a large boulder. There is a shallow left leaning trough which intersects this route near the ledge.

38. Church Not Made By Hands 10c At the right end of the wall are two parallel cracks in front of a large dead tree. Start in the right crack which eventually bends left (crux and prayer station) to meet another crack. Follow that one to the top.

Gorilla Rock is located to the left (west) of Granite Stairway. The usual approach consists of bushwhacking up the trail indicated in Fig. 9.2. The next climb, oriented at 200°, is found on the southwest side of the crag .

39. Still A Gorilla 11d Climb up a thin crack found under and just left of a protruding block. After about 20 feet (near a T junction), go right 5 feet under the protruding block, pass the short overhang via a finger crack and on to the top where you can beat your breast Tarzan style. See Fig. 9.1.

There are two prominent alcoves on the north face which can be reached by scrambling through piled up boulders on the northwest end. Both alcoves are shown in Fig. 9.10. A blocky summit sits on top of the left side of the face. There is a down sloping shelf to the right of this summit. A rappel station is at the top of the left (east) alcove. *Gash* is an orientation climb for this alcove.

40. Slash 10a This climb consists of a slightly bulging hand crack that is a few feet left of *Gash*. It ends at the down sloping shelf.

41. Gash 10b Start in an offwidth located below the junction of the blocky summit and the down sloping shelf. The offwidth transforms into a finger and hand crack as you move up the line.

42. Bad Girls Do 10b Just to the right of *Gash,* follow another wide crack that is not as wide as the next climb.

43. Bad Girl's Dream 11b This is the rightmost of 4 obvious climbs. It's a big, bad offwidth with an overhanging awkward start.

The rightmost (west) alcove contains two climbs. The descent is from a rappel station at the top of the alcove.

Figure 9.10   Gorilla Rock, North Face.

44. Gloria's Fantasy 10b An easier version of the next climb. If you fantasize about offwidths, do you need therapy?

45. Gloria 11b An offwidth climb with the crux *in excelsis* (high up).

46. Garden of Earthly Delights 11c Find four bolts on the west face of the blocky summit to the left of a wide crack. Follow them to the top. (*Erratum*: Routes 45 and 46 are mislabeled in Fig. 9.2 as Routes 40 and 42 respectively.)

Westworld, H and I Crag, and Parade Rock

Westworld lies to the north of Gorilla Rock across a small valley. It is accessible by the trails shown in Fig. 9.2. There are two established routes on the crag towards the right end of the southeast side. Descent is by walkoff.

47. Date With a Dike 10d Ascend a prominent right leaning dike with three bolts en route on a wall facing 170°. Only the politically incorrect would comment on the name of this route given by the first ascensionist (a male).

48. Pollyanna Goes To Hell 11a Start 5 yards right of *Date* and climb a chimney to a vertical and partially detached flake. Protect it well, lest you go to Hell.

H and I Crag is the name of the next crag which, coincidentally, is indicated as "H" in Fig. 9.2 (see this Figure for access). It's located directly north and across a small saddle from Granite Staircase. There are only two known routes, both on the south side of this formation. There is potential for other new ascents. Descent is from a rappel station at the top of *I*. See Fig. 9.11.

49. H 10c Find the prominent roof at the left end of the southwest face. Climb to the roof via a crack that lies beneath roof. Pass the roof on the right.

50. I 11b Start 10 yards right of *H*. Climb a strenuous fingers/off fingers line that leans to the right and is oriented at 210° (a.k.a. *Animal Cracker Land*)

Parade Rock, basically a huge boulder, has two established routes on it. It can be reached from the east or west by the trails shown in Fig. 9.2. Given its isolated location you will be the only attraction as the deer parade by. See Fig. 9.12.

51. Parade Rest 9 Begin in a right facing dihedral located near the right end of the southwest side. Climb the offwidth start and finish on an excellent hand crack.

52. Soft Parade 11c Worth the walk. Proceed about 5 yards right from *Parade Rest* to a wall facing 150°. Climb a splendid bulging, finger crack. Tread softly and leave no traces.

Figure 9.11 H and I Crag, North Face.

Figure 9.12 Parade Rock

Spelunk Spire, End of the Road, and Devil's Playground

Spelunk Spire was definitely visited by the hard men of earlier times who named it. Old ironmongery and other remnants of their exploratory forays are occasionally to be found here. The name ostensibly comes from the myriad of caves and tunnels formed by the jumbled boulders that must be negotiated on the south side of the main spire and which served as the start of the original summit route, *Spelunk Spiral*. Only 5 climbs have been documented here. However, others probably exist and more certainly will. See Fig. 9.2 for location.

53. Sky Shot 11a This route is located at the top (northwest end) of the formation and begins below the main spire on the left side of a large undercut. Pass the roof on the left using a good hand jam. The crack then thins as two old and questionable pitons are passed. However, the crack widens near the top. This route can be done in one pitch using a standard rack supplemented by a couple of extra big pieces for near the end. Descent is by somewhat demanding downclimbing on the backside (southwest side) of the spire.

The next route is approximately 100 yards before (north) of the southwest end of the spire. It's located on the lower southwest portion of the formation near a large pine tree.

54. Wrist Ranger 8+ This route, which starts as a 40 foot handcrack, is located on a northwest facing wall. A distinguishing characteristic is a right leaning dike that crosses the crack about two thirds the way up. After the crack, finish on unprotected 5.5 face. Walk off.

55. Paper Training 9 This right facing dihedral is 20 yards right of *Wrist* . Walk Off.

56. The Old Dog's New Trick 11c This very thin finger crack is found at the southwest end. The protection is meager on this climb. Top roping is recommended if you want to live to be an old dog.

57. Spelunk Spiral 2 Start on the southeast side and scramble up through the boulder field, eventually funneling into the eastern chimney to finish.

Several interesting and varied climbs are found on the south side of End of the Road Rock. To get there cross a fence line via a ladder stair bridge. Middle Crow Creek will be on your right. A very large roof will be above you immediately to the left. See Figs. 9.13 and 9.14. Descent for all climbs is a scramble to the top and a downclimb to the northeast. Two prominent lines can be seen on the southeast side. Only the right one is known to have been climbed.

Figure 9.13 End of Road Rock, Southeast Face.

Figure 9.14 End of Road Rock, East Face.

Figure 9.15 Devil's Playground.

58. Proctologist 11c Ascend the right crack and finish in a left facing dihedral. Be careful at the pod (crux), or you could end up with a stone proctoscopy.

There is a large blocky pillar (BP) about 10 yards right of *Proctologist*. It is detached from the main formation and forms a hallway. The next two climbs are found inside the hallway. See Fig. 9.14.

59. Inside Straight 9+ A handcrack that is deceptively overhung is found on the outside wall of the hallway. Take extra hand size camming units.

60. Inside Flush 10b Just across the hallway from *Inside Straight*, this crack is found on the inside wall, i.e., on the main crag itself. It is similar to *Inside Straight* but has a surprising and flaring offwidth finish.

61. Two of a Kind 9 There are twin cracks just right of the hallway. Use these textbook hand cracks simultaneously.

62. Poker Face 10c Aptly named, as the difficulties can't be ascertained by outward appearances. To the right of the preceding 3 climbs is a southeast facing wall. A huge wedge of boulder forms a right leaning crack on its right side. Climb the crack. You win the pot if you maintain a straight face as you strain on the sustained fists.

Devil's Playground has been virtually unexploited by free climbers -- maybe scared off by the name and its isolated position across Middle Crow Creek. However, Joe Wieder claimed he did the first ascent of *Muscle and Fitness* in 1972. However, rumor has it that local crack master, Bob Scarpelli, actually did the first redpoint of this excellent route somewhat later. Who knows? The climb is on the north face. See Fig. 9.15.

63. Muscle and Fitness 11c Approach from the right (west) via an upward slanting ramp. Climb through an overhanging roof, and move left into a strenuous right arching offwidth. Top out and belay from a shelf above the offwidth. The fitness training occurs when you try to pull your second up.

To climb smoothly between sky and earth,
in a succession of precise and efficient movements,
induces an inner peace and even a mood of gaiety,
it is like a well-regulated ballet,
with the roped climbers all in their respective places.
Gaston Rebuffat

Figure 10.1 The Vertical Dance

10. BLAIR

Blair is a wonderful northwest extension of Vedauwoo--a complex set of crags that has been climbed on as long as the Central Area. However, for over 20 years no guidebook has included it so most visitors seldom climb there. To get to Blair, use the South Blair Road which runs parallel to and south of I-80. If coming from the east, take the Vedauwoo exit and instead of heading into the Central Area on Route 700, go the opposite direction (southwest) for a short distance and turn right (northwest) onto South Blair Road. After 1.8 miles turn right onto Route 705. If coming from the west, take the Lincoln Monument turnoff. Instead of turning left into the Monument, go right onto the South Blair Road. Continue on South Blair Road for 4 miles and turn left on Route 705. At 1.5 miles along Route 705, the Eight Ball is visible at 09:30 and the Three Blairs (called Brady Rock on the Geological Survey Map) at 11:30. John's Tower is to the right of the Eight Ball, while the Heap appears in the background between John's Tower and the Three Blairs. The Five Corners area lies between the Heap and Blair III. There is a picnic turnoff at 2.3 miles--the place to park for climbing at the Three Blairs. Take a trail heading east from the picnic area. After a quarter of a mile, you arrive at the southwest end of Blair III. Getting to Blair II and Blair I from there is obvious. Use Figs. 10.2 and 10.3 for a topographic overview.

> *SpectreMan 11c ...* **a splendid hand crack. 70 feet of perfection. Overhanging with perfect jams and good stemming**

LOWER BLAIR

BLAIR I and EXTENSIONS

The next route is on the northwest side about a third of the way from the northeast end of the formation. Descend by scrambling to the southwest.

1. Raised On Robbery 10b Start in an A-frame nook, and climb out of it to follow a right leaning hand/fist crack through a couple of overhangs to the top.

On the southeast side of Blair I is a high gully with an extension of rock projecting southeast past the gully. The next two routes are on this extension. Descend by scrambling back towards the high gully. See Fig. 10.4.

2. When You're Strange 11b There is a large aspen tree 14 yards left of *Bat Drop Crack*. Begin in a short left facing dihedral in front of the tree, and surmount a roof leading to a thin, flaring crack. Struggle to a little ledge on the left at which

BLAIR

THE HEAP

SPECTREMAN BUTTRESS (behind N. Corner)

CURREY'S CORNER

SOUTH CORNER

THE SHERMAN MOUNTAINS

MOBY DICK

LITTLE BLAIR

JOHN'S TOWER

NORTH CORNER

EAST CORNER

ADAM'S RIB III

BLAIR III

BLAIR II

BLAIR I

THE 8 BALL

LITTLE JOHN'S TOWER

PRINCIPAL FORMATIONS
Viewed From Road 705
Looking Approximately Northeast

Figure 10.2

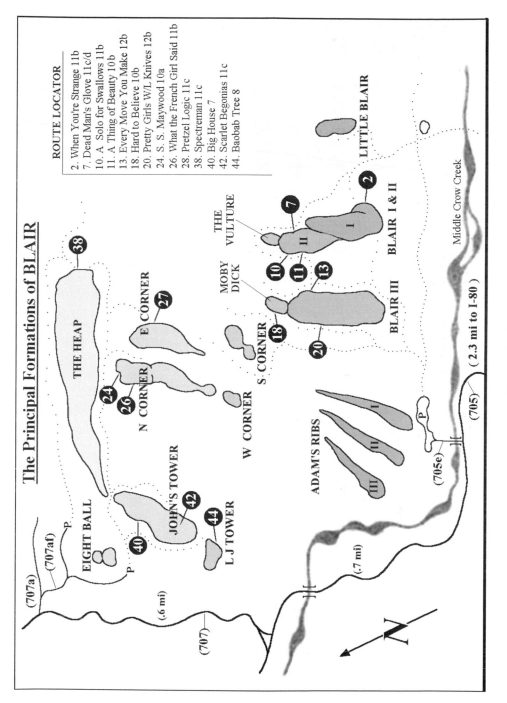

The Principal Formations of BLAIR

ROUTE LOCATOR

2. When You're Strange 11b
7. Dead Man's Glove 11c/d
10. A Solo for Swallows 11b
11. A Thing of Beauty 10b
13. Every Move You Make 12b
18. Hard to Believe 10b
20. Pretty Girls W/L Knives 12b
24. S. S. Maywood 10a
26. What the French Girl Said 11b
28. Pretzel Logic 11c
38. Spectreman 11c
40. Big House 7
42. Scarlet Begonias 11c
44. Baobab Tree 8

THE HEAP

EIGHT BALL

JOHN'S TOWER

L J TOWER

N CORNER

E CORNER

W CORNER

S CORNER

MOBY DICK

THE VULTURE

BLAIR I & II

BLAIR III

LITTLE BLAIR

ADAM'S RIBS

Middle Crow Creek

(707a)

(707af)

(.6 mi)

(707)

(.7 mi)

(705e)

(705)

(2.3 mi to I-80)

N

Figure 10.3

point the crack widens to fists and offwidth.

3.   Bat Drop Crack 10b At the right end of the extension is a right angle dihedral (left wall faces northeast and right wall 110°). The left wall is low angle with a vertical paint brush of lichen. Start in the dihedral, traverse left onto the face to avoid the bat guano, and follow a thin crack to the top.

High atop the southeast side of Blair I is a notch along the left side of the skyline.

4.   Little Creatures 11b Scramble up the high gully to the crack below the notch. Climb the crack (easy). Move right and climb the dihedral corner to the right of the notch--hands to wider than hands.

The distinctive and isolated Little Blair formation is a couple of hundred yards southeast from the middle of Blair I.

5.   Blair Blaster 9 Climb the obvious crack line on the northwest face passing a roof along the way.

A quarter mile southeast of the Vulture is a small formation with a flat 45 foot high wall that faces northwest. In the middle of the wall is a distinctive crack that originates behind a flake, slants left, and then goes vertical.

6.   Stress Fracture 10b Follow that crack and finish on a sloping shelf.

BLAIR II

The Vulture is a befittingly named, very large, flat, standing boulder on the northeast end of Blair II. The next route is on the east side of Blair II just left of the notch formed between the main body of the crag and the Vulture. Descent is by downclimbing the notch on the northwest side.

7.   Deadman's Glove 11c Start in a right facing dihedral, and then traverse right onto a northeast face as the route follows 4 bolts to an easy, wide crack exit.

The following routes begin on the northwest side of the crag. They are right of the notch between the Vulture and the main body of the crag. See Fig. 10.5.

8.   Good-bye White Opel 11b [*sic*] Climb the right side of the right wall between Vulture and the main body of the crag (low fifth class). Traverse right along a ledge for a few yards to a right leaning crack that starts as a thin slot, opens a bit, and then closes off near the top as it comes to a ledge. Finish in a short handcrack in a left facing dihedral. The protection is dicey, and RP's are useful near the crux.

Figure 10.4 Blair I, Blair II, and the Vulture, Southeast Face.

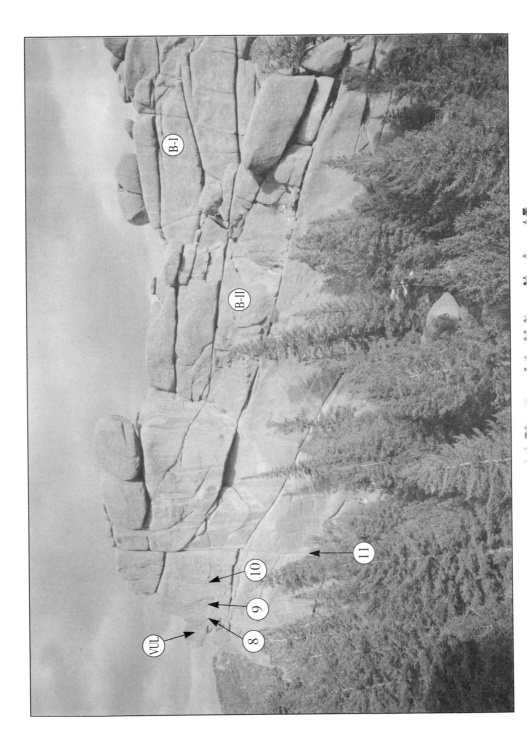

9. Medium Cool 10d Five yards right of *Opel* is a straight up finger to hand crack that shares the exit of *Opel*.

10. Solo For Swallows 11b Start in a groove 10 yards past the start of the *Medium Cool*. The groove leads to a thin crack and then to a pod. Next comes a thin left facing dihedral (crux) which leads to a ledge. Finish on another thin 5.11 crack.

11. A Thing of Beauty 10b Aptly named--a stunning line. The northwest wall of Blair II is furrowed down the middle by a prominent crack in front of a big pine tree. The lower two thirds is a hand crack in a right facing dihedral, whereas the last section is a straight in offwidth. Since the crack does not extend to the ground, approach from the right along a ledge. The climbing then starts above the beginning of the crack. There is a direct 11b start, basically unprotectable, straight up to the crack.

BLAIR III and MOBY DICK

There is a large notch near the northeast end of Blair III . Past the northeast end of the notch is a huge oblong block of rock called Moby Dick (MD). It has the right shape for Herman Melville's whale, if not the right color.

A principal landmark on the southeast side of Blair III is a huge flange of rock pointing due east and topped by a boulder projecting out in a 10 foot ceiling. It lies 15 yards left of the notch between Moby Dick and the main body of Blair III. The flange touches an arete on the right end of a huge projecting flake that forms a shield in front of the main body of the crag. For the next 4 routes descend by downclimbing the notch on the northwest side. See Fig. 10.6.

12. Balls Out 11a Begin in a groove at the left end of the shield, struggling up to a thin crack (Lowe Balls near the start). After reaching a headwall go left, then traverse back right (8+), and finish in a great 5.9 handcrack.

13. Every Move You Make 12b Begin twenty yards right of *Balls Out* on a thin, vexatious face leading to a left leaning crack that goes all the way to the top through a series of bulges. Near the top the crack widens considerably (a.k.a. *Gambit*).

14. Arete Aready 10a Start in crack about 3 yards left of the arete at the right end of the shield. Ascend 40 feet to a horizontal crack, traverse right, and follow the bolts on the next route to the top. (The first ascent was done prior to the bolts being in place.)

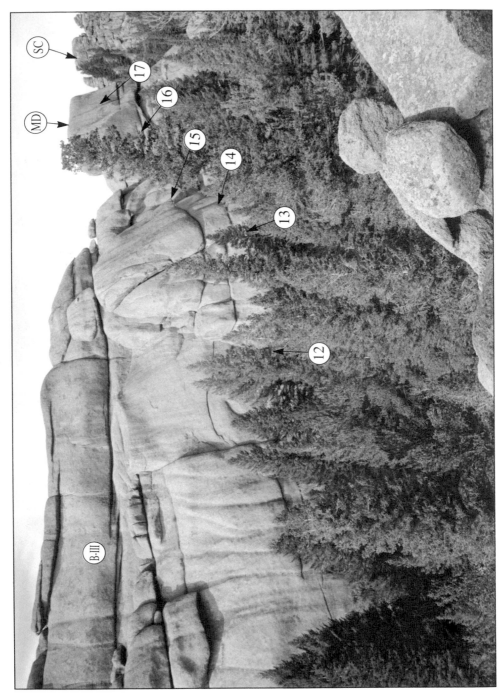

Figure 10.6. Blair II and Moby Dick, Southeast Face.

15. Bragging About Jesus 10a A line of 10 bolts leads up the arete. This is a good climb, but it's tricky getting to the bolts without having your rope jam. One option is to carry the rope with you and work your way through the chimney in the back until you are able to step out to the first bolt. At that point, throw one end of the rope to your belayer (assuming he's still there; otherwise throw both ends down). A medium camming device can be placed in the horizontal crack about two thirds the way up.

The southeast face of Moby Dick is creased by 2 cracks--the first about a third of the way from the left end, while the second is a third of the way from the right end. There is a faint, right leaning crack between them.

16. Damit 8 This is the crack on the left. Approach from the left via a slanting ramp. Start in a right facing dihedral that changes to left facing. The crack becomes wide at the top. There are rappel chains at the end. The original route, from the 1960's, traversed right from this point to finish on the middle crack.

17. The Putter 10b This is the crack on the right. Traverse in from the left or from the northwest side (original route). Climb the offwidth/hand crack to the top. Descend as in *Damit* (a.k.a. *A Horse Will Have To Do*).

Moby Dick is split on its northwest side by the conspicuous offwidth crack, *Hard To Believe.*

18. Hard To Believe 10b Traverse in from the right along a ledge to access the offwidth. The route is very sustained with a crux near the slight jog in the middle. Descend as for *Damit.*

19. Outer Notch 7 The wall on the right side of the notch faces northeast. Climb to the top via the cluster of cracks on the right side of the wall, passing through a slot near the end.

The next two climbs are found are on the northwest face of Blair III. See Fig. 10.7.

20. Pretty Girls With Long Knives 12b This enticing, sustained line is found near the middle of the crag. There are two large trees, one alive and one dead, standing in front of it. Start in a left facing dihedral and then follow a thin, arching crack that characterizes the climb. The crux comes near the top of the arch past which there is a ledge. Finish on a hand/fist crack above the ledge. Descend by downclimbing the notch on the northwest side.

21. Intimidation 9+ This route starts 90 yards from the southwest end of the crag in a very small triangular slot. It is a right leaning hand/fist crack that sinu-

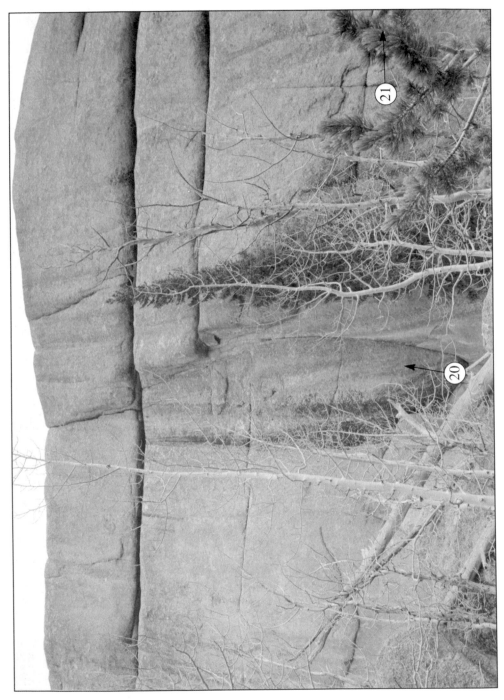

Figure 10.7 Blair III. Northwest Face.

Figure 10.8 Paul Piana. First Ascent of *Pretty Girls with Long Knives (12b).*
Photograph courtesy of Piana/Cowboyography.

ously weaves its way up through a series of ledges. Descend by scrambling to the southwest end.

UPPER BLAIR

You can walk from the lower picnic area to the Upper Blair Area, or drive 0.7 mile past the picnic area and turn right on Route 707. Continue for a little more than half a mile and turn right onto Route 707AF. Park shortly after that. From this vantage point, The Eight Ball, John's Tower and the Heap are clearly visible. There are faint trails leading to all of the formations, but when they become too obscure, bushwhacking will get you where you want to go. Refer to Figs. 10.2 and 10.3.

THE FIVE CORNERS

This area lies in the heart of Blair--south of The Heap and west of John's Tower. Approach along the south side of The Heap or by hiking up along the northwest side of Blair III. The most developed crag is North Corner which is identifiable by a boulder shaped like a Hershey Kiss on its top. The Kiss is easily seen when viewed from the west and appears on the left side of the crag. Middle Corner is to the right of The Kiss and across a gap. West Corner is much farther to the right and across a bigger gap. *S.S. Maywood* is the best route for orientation on North Corner (Fig. 10.9). It lies on the northwest end at the center of a great, big dihedral. The left wall faces northwest and the right wall slightly east of north. The next route is around the corner to the left of *S.S. Maywood* and face northeast.

22. Easter Island 12a Follow a line of gold shut bolts to a seam, and go left at a T-crack above a dike aiming for the rappel bolts.

23. Jihad 11d There is a crack angling left on the left side of the left wall of the S.S. Maywood Dihedral. Climb easy, but unprotected, face to the crack. Continue as it crosses to the northeast face. Follow the crack as it arches up.

24. S.S. Maywood 10a Approach from the right and climb the spine of the huge dihedral. A great place to be if it's hot.

Two parallel cracks, which begin on a shelf, are high up on the northwest wall right of the S.S. Maywood dihedral. The crack on the right continues down to a lower shelf.

25. Calling On You, Moscow 11b Start by climbing the lower part of the crack in the next route, and belay below the crack on the left. Ascend this: fingers to thin hands to a bulge to more fingers finishing in a left facing dihedral.

Figure 10.9 The climbs at North Corner.

Figure 10.10   East Corner. Southwest Face.

26. What the French Girl Said 11b Approach from the right along the lower ramp, and climb the right crack which is very thin at the bottom and flaring hands at the top.

The next two routes are on southeast side of East Corner. There is a prominent roof left of center on this side of the crag. *Pretzel Logic* begins directly beneath this roof. See Fig. 10.10. Descent is a downclimb to the southwest.

27. Tips and Asps 11c Begin 8 yards left of *Pretzel Logic.* Traverse in from the left under a roof. Climb to a pod, continue to a shelf, and finish on vertical cracks.

28. Pretzel Logic 11c Climb a hand crack to a roof on the right. Continue to the large, left facing dihedral. Turn the big roof on the right.

THE HEAP

Despite the undignified name, the routes on this crag are classic. See Fig. 10.11. *SpectreMan* is surely one of the very best hand cracks at Vedauwoo. The established routes are at the east end of the crag. Use the parking lot for John's Tower, and hike along the south side of The Heap. Alternatively, pull off left shortly after getting on Route 707AF, and park at the end of the road. Then hike along the north side of The Heap. The principal orienting feature is the southeast face of SpectreMan Buttress at the east end of the crag. The wall is about 20 yards wide and bounded at either end by 2 flanges of rock. *SpectreMan* occupies the dihedral corner formed by the flange at the right end. Moving left (clockwise) from this wall, you come to a wall facing 160°. There are two vertical cracks on this wall which is splattered with dikes. Descend from chains atop *Call Me Barney* for the next 3 climbs.

29. Mystery Blocks(?) 11d Follow 3 bolts up the dike studded face finishing off a little to the right at the top of the next route.

30. Call Me Barney 11c Start in a slot and climb the thin crack on the left. Rappel bolts.

31. The Rookie 12a Flash this and get the Rookie of the Year award. Climb the crack on the right starting in a left facing dihedral.

On the tier above *Call Me Barney* is a blocky formation with several cracks facing between south and southeast. Over the years they've all received several first ascents and many different names. The following are the oldest names we could find.

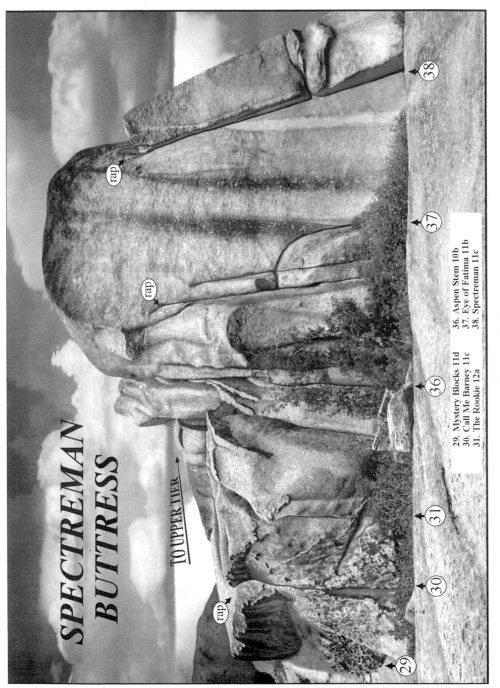

SPECTREMAN BUTTRESS

TO UPPER TIER →

rap

29. Mystery Blocks 11d
30. Call Me Barney 11c
31. The Rookie 12a

36. Aspen Stem 10b
37. Eye of Fatima 11b
38. Spectreman 11c

Figure 10.11

Figure 10.12 Steve Bechtel on Mystery Blocks (?) (11d)

32. My Clone Sleeps Alone 10a This crack starts at the left end of the block in a small right facing dihedral.

33. Rubber Biscuit 10a Start a few yards right in a left facing dihedral.

34. Storm Watch 10a Around a bulge is another crack in a right facing dihedral.

35. Flip, Flop, and Die 10a Start a few yards right of *Storm Watch* in a crack in a left facing dihedral.

The next climb starts at the lower level in a slot just left of *Fatima*.

36. Aspen Stem 11a Climb the middle crack in the slot (8) starting between 2 aspen trees. Belay on a ledge after 40 feet. Then squeeze past the flaring off-width on the left (crux) and follow the crack to a platform as the climbing eases up.

There are rappel stations atop the next 2 climbs, both of which are about 60 feet long.

37. Eye of Fatima 11b Climb the left crack on SpectreMan Wall.

38. SpectreMan 11c Super Classic. Climb the right crack on the SpectreMan Wall.

39. Behind Blue Eyes 11b A good climb that's hard to find. There is a small crag about 200 hundred yards slightly east of south from SpectreMan Wall. It is in a ravine and surrounded by aspen trees. Find a dihedral on its east side, and climb the thin crack which sports two bolts.

JOHN'S TOWER and LITTLE JOHN'S TOWER

The next two climbs are on the north side of John's Tower (JT). See Fig. 10.13

40. Big House 7 Climb the manifest wide crack that bisects the north face.

41. Becker 6 Begin in the left of two parallel cracks on the buttress at the right end of the wall. At the top of the buttress, traverse to a crack on the right and follow it to the top.

The next two climbs are on the south side of John's Tower near the left end. See Fig. 10.14.

Figure 10.13   John's Tower, Northwest Face

Figure 10.14.   John's Tower and Little John's Tower Southeast Faces.

42. Scarlet Begonias 11c As viewed from the ground, this is the leftmost of 3 cracks on the upper tier and finishes at a little notch in the skyline. Approach from the left. The climb actually begins in a chimney and then goes fingers to bulge to offwidth slot.

43. Ultra Violets 10d A well-defined right angle dihedral corner is to the right of the 3 cracks just mentioned. It's at the right end of the ramp, and its right face is oriented southwest. Ascend the dihedral, and exit through the monstrous crack on the bulging roof on the right.

The last climb in this section is on the south face of Little John's Tower (LJT). The upper part of the face is split by a conspicuous crack in a right facing dihedral.

44. Baobab Tree 8 Come up from the right to the base of the crack and climb it. Descend by scrambling down the north side.

11. The Citadel Area

How to get away from it all and still be there. Consider the Citadel Area which is an "outlying" area less than 15 minutes from Central Vedauwoo. It contains mostly short, hard routes that offer special challenges to the experienced climber. We highlight a few extraordinary climbs from the many that have been ascended and remain to be ascended. To get to the Citadel Area, drive two miles north from the Central Area Turnoff. Turn right (west) on Route 700C and park after 0.6 miles. See Fig. 11.1. The Citadel Area can be conveniently divided into 4 subareas: Plumb Line Crag, Short Wall, Citadel Proper, and Worm Drive Crag. They are clustered about one another and within a 15 minute hiking distance in a southwesterly direction from the parking area. The next three climbs are shown in Fig. 11.2. The first two are on a wall facing 200°.

Plumb Line Crag

1. Big Pink 11b Climb the considerably overhanging offwidth on the left end of the south facing, lower tier.

2. Plumb Line 9 This is a plum of a line. Climb the textbook handcrack found 4 yards right of *Pink*.

3. June Bride 12a This climb is a bit difficult to locate. It can be found in the amphitheater part of Plum Line Crag on a steep, southeast facing slab. It's a considerable distance to the right from *Plumb Line*. The route follows a very thin line that accepts RP's, small stoppers, and maybe a TCU.

The Short Wall

The formation is located approximately 150 yards southeast of the Plumb Line Amphitheater. The lower tier has two classic offwidths and a finger/hand crack as shown in Fig. 11.3. The upper tier to the right is a monolithic finger of granite with a spectacular, exposed 11c on its southeast face. See Fig. 11.4. This structure can also be seen intermittently through the trees on your right as you drive in on Route 700C. The next three climbs are on the lower tier which faces 160°. Descent is by walkoff in any convenient direction.

4. Jay's Solo 10c Within 30 feet of overhang you have: hands to fist to off fist. What more could you ask for?

5. Misfits 11a This starts a couple of yards right of *Jay's*. It's thin up into the incut where you must surmount an overhung roof that provides the crux finish.

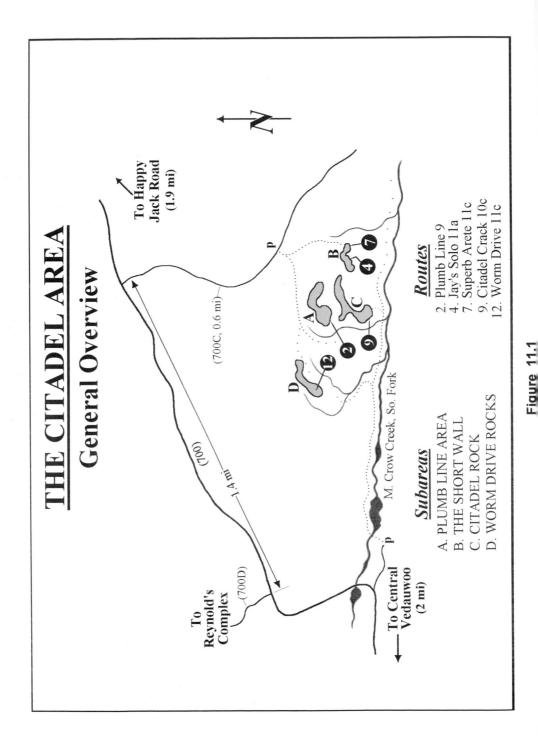

Figure 11.1

Figure 11.2 The Plumb Line Crag.

Figure 11.3 Short Wall, Lower Tier.

Figure 11.4 Short Wall, Upper Tier.

6. Drees Special 11c Start a few yards right of *Misfits*. Ascend a left leaning crack. The lean is mean on this one.

The next two climbs are on the upper tier and a little to the right (east) of the lower tier climbs. Descent is from rappel bolts on the top.

7. Superb Arete 11c This visionary line with 3 bolts is highly recommended. It has a breath taking start with immediate and continuous exposure.

8. Who Knows 9 A single bolt protects this otherwise unprotectable face climb.

THE CITADEL PROPER

This area is south of Plumb Line Crag and west of the Short Wall. Descent is by downclimbing to the north. The next two routes are on the southwest end of the crag. See Fig. 11.5. *Heads* is an easy climb to orient by because of its distinctive right leaning dike.

9. Citadel Crack 10b The namesake climb for the whole area and worthily so. There is a big slot just left of the start of *Heads,* and a projecting roof is just left of the slot. Start in a handcrack a few yards further left. Climb to a small roof which is larger on the right than the left. Continue up the crack which is now the spine of a left facing dihedral whose right face is formed by a projecting flange. Pass one more small roof on the way to the top.

10. Heads of the Valley 9+ The route faces due south. Climb with your head screwed on right as you move up the right leaning dike that diagonals across the right side of the wall. The protection is meager so proceed with caution.

The last route we list on this crag is on the northwest side as shown in Fig. 11.6.

11. Castles in the Sand 11b Climb to piton and then follow the bolts on this neat face climb.

WORM DRIVE CRAG

The last two climbs that we have selected from the Citadel Area are each very worthwhile undertakings. The contorted wiggling required on *Worm* will be especially enticing for the offwidth enthusiast. See Fig. 11.7.

12. Worm Drive 11b The climb faces southeast and starts in a 10 foot high slot that ends in a roof. An offwidth shaft springs forth from the left end of the roof. The name aptly describes the corkscrew maneuvers that you'll need to ascend the shaft.

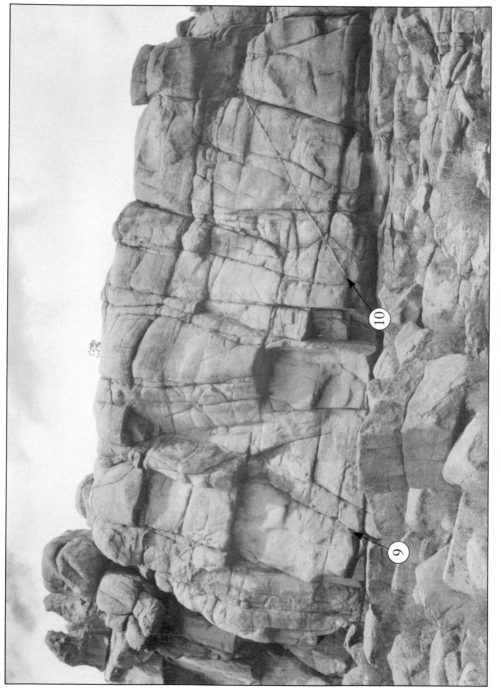

Figure 11.5 The Citadel, West Face.

Figure 11.6 The Citadel, Northwest Face.

Figure 11.7 Worm Drive Rocks.

13. First Gear 8 Start 8 yards right of *Worm* in an open slot and ascend a left facing dihedral. Pass on the right a small roof and finish on a crack that faces southwest.

12. Happy Jack Road

Happy Jack Road is a cheerful, northern outreach of Vedauwoo. Although there has been a lot of climbing here over the years, the area has the aura of being totally undeveloped and most of its routes remain unrecorded. We provide here a sampler of some of the better known climbs in the area. Refer to map inside front cover for orientation.

The Roof Ranch

To get to the Roof Ranch go left (west) about 3 miles from the intersection of Route 700 and Happy Jack Road. Turn right (north) onto Route 701 and bear right to continue for about a mile on Route 701E. You can see the top of the formation above the trees as you look to the left. Just hike towards the rocks. Roof Ranch consists of two separate crags quite close to each other. As the area is approached from the parking spot, the Bunk House is on the left (north) and Roof Ranch proper is on the right (south). The Bunk House has two excellent climbs as shown in Fig. 12.1.

1. Emperor of Wyoming 11a Start near the left end of the formation. Climb a wide crack in a right facing dihedral that becomes left facing and leads to a little shelf. Continue in the left facing dihedral, and pass on the right the roof that looms above. Continue to the top.

2. Rising Sun 11b Start about 4 yards left of the right end of the formation. This route is to the right of the large fissure in the middle of the formation. After a small bit of face climbing, ascend a strenuous, bulging finger crack which lies in a groove. There is a small pod a little before the angle eases over.

One look at it, and you'll have no doubt why the Roof Ranch has been given its name. It includes three of the best and most technically difficult roofs in Greater Vedauwoo. See Figs. 12.2. There is a rappel station at the top of *Moonsault* which serves all the remaining climbs. The first two climbs below are found on a distinct northwest facing wall to the left of *Moonsault.* There is a slot between Roof Ranch and the Bunk House. These two climbs are found on the right just as the gully starts becoming steeper. They are not of the same heroic character as the remaining routes on the crag, but don't be fooled. At their level of difficulty, they are more than interesting.

3. Lichen or Not 7+ Climb the crack system in a left facing dihedral. Move over large flakes and surmount a bulge to the top. A bit runout.

Figure 12.1 The Roof Ranch, Bunk House.

Figure 12.2 The Roof Ranch

4. **Lichentous Wall 9+** This starts a yard or so to the right of *Lichen* and basically follows a shallow groove past some bulges. Gear: take some Lowe Balls.

The dominating features on the west face of the wall are two, big horizontal roofs with the upper one about 10 feet above the lower roof.

5. **Moonsault 11c** Start in the crack in a right facing dihedral below the left end of the lower roof. Follow the very strenuous finger crack around the bulge to the balcony. Now follow the finger crack above you past the second roof. Belay at a rappel station.

6. **Flying Ants 11d** This is an alternate and demanding exit to *Moonsault.* When you get to the balcony in the middle of *Moonsault,* walk to the right. Climb the next finger crack going through the upper roof.

7. **Squat 12b** This is a remarkable, short test piece which probably has not received a second ascent. It makes little sense to say that a 12b offwidth is underrated, but that may be the case here. Walk right about 10 yards from the start of *Moonsault,* and find an offwidth leading to roof. There will be two bolts. Start in a right facing dihedral and continue through the roof.

CAMP JACK ROCKS

To get to Camp Jack go east about 1.9 miles along the Happy Jack Road from its intersection with Route 700, and then turn left (north) onto Camp Jack Road. Sometimes there is a sign here with the name Camp Jack on it but not always. Proceed for about a mile and park. The Camp Jack Rocks will be to the north across Brush Creek. As will be evident, they consist of three related formations. The area has been known for years, mostly because of one excellent climb, *Jet Stream*, which is located on the northwest face of the westmost and largest formation. It has been something of a local secret for years. Descent for all these climbs is a walkoff to either side. See Figs. 12.3 and 12.4.

Attention: Do not use North Creek Road, which lies west of Camp Jack Road and west of the Camp Jack Rocks, as an approach to this area, since it requires crossing private property. Such trespassing could jeopardize future access to this area.

Attention: Camp Jack Rocks are not in Albany County and Medicine Bow National Forest. They are in Laramie County and on State of Wyoming land. Note that the City of Cheyenne is in Laramie County, whereas the City of Laramie is in Albany County. For emergency services here, call 911. Otherwise, contact Albany County Sheriff's Office, 1910 Pioneer Ave., Cheyenne WY 82001, Telephone (non-emergency): (307)633-4700. The hospital in Cheyenne is : United

Figure 12.3 Camp Jack Rocks, West Main Formation, Northwest Face.

Figure 12.4 Camp Jack Rocks, West Formation, West Face.

Medical Center, 300 E. 23rd St., Cheyenne WY 82001, Telephone (non-emergency): (307)634-3341

8. Jet Stream 9 Scramble up to a crack in the middle of the face, and enjoy perfect hand jams on an exquisite, exposed crack line.

The remaining climbs are shown in Fig. 12.4 and will be found on the west face of the main (westmost) formation.

9. Fever Dreams 11a Almost a boulder problem. A little left of *Giggle*, an arching crack slants up beneath a roof on the right. The climb mostly presents thin, overhanging stemming.

10. Giggle 8 This is a really neat climb with exposed jamming high up on the crag. Get to the climb by scrambling up from the left. Ascend a crack line up the face forming the right side of the dihedral to the right of *Fever*. Rumor has it that there is a 5.6 first pitch.

11. Give Me a Second, I'll Think of Something 10a Start in left facing dihedral, diagonal up and right to a ledge. Move slightly right to a vertical hand crack that becomes a finger crack as you move up.

12. The Slant 9 Towards the right end of the face, find a right leaning hand crack in right facing dihedral. It makes a T-junction after 25 feet. Go right at that point along a sloping ledge.

13. Tick List Ordered by Rating

We give a "tick list" where the routes are grouped by difficulty. This should be useful for Type A climbers as well as Type B's who want an overview of climbs at a given level of difficulty. A histogram of route frequency is shown in Fig. 13-1. It is not at all surprising that the number of routes peaks at 5.9, after all this is about the middle of the range. Also, 5.9 has tended historically to be a generic rating, often encompassing climbs harder than 5.7 but less difficult than 10d. However, it is surprising that there is a decline in the number of routes at 10c and 10d and then a sharp rise at 11a and 11b. Our own guess is that this more reflects the psychology of climbers than it does a natural phenomenon inherent in the structure of the crags. Stated more simply, this may be an example of grade inflation. Namely, once a climb gets to the hard end of 5.10, there is a distinctly human tendency on the part of the first ascensionist to think that the route belongs in the next grade. It doesn't hurt the ego of those who follow to agree with this grade. The authors are well aware of this temptation.

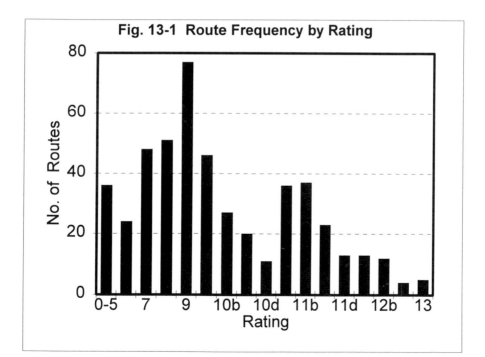

Fig. 13-1 Route Frequency by Rating

ROUTES BY RATING

5.0 to 5.5

- ☐ Baldwin's Chimney
- ☐ Clam Shell
- ☐ Colostemmy
- ☐ Corbel Exit
- ☐ Cornelius
- ☐ Drain Pipe
- ☐ E.O. Lieback
- ☐ E.O.Friction
- ☐ East Face
- ☐ Easy Jam
- ☐ Edwards' Crack--Left Exit
- ☐ Edwards' Crack--Right Exit
- ☐ Etude For The Left Hand
- ☐ Etude For The Right Hand
- ☐ Foolishness
- ☐ Glenda's Chimney
- ☐ Glenn's First Name
- ☐ Hide-A-Way Chimney
- ☐ Jake's Variation
- ☐ Left Exit
- ☐ Left Start
- ☐ Little Old Crack
- ☐ Low Road
- ☐ Parabolic Slab Route
- ☐ Petite Tarsalation
- ☐ Powder Puff
- ☐ Practice Chimney
- ☐ Right Parallel Space
- ☐ Sisca Face
- ☐ Soft Touch
- ☐ Southwest Friction
- ☐ Spelunk Spiral
- ☐ Sunny Day
- ☐ Tourist Trap
- ☐ Up the Down Chimney
- ☐ Walt's Wall Route

5.6

- ☐ Barf Bucket Traverse
- ☐ Becker
- ☐ Bill Steal
- ☐ Black Starr Chimney
- ☐ Bushwhack
- ☐ Cave Crack
- ☐ Croissant
- ☐ H&H Grunt
- ☐ Horticulture
- ☐ Joke
- ☐ Kim
- ☐ Left Femur
- ☐ Like Fun
- ☐ Maiden
- ☐ Moor Crossing
- ☐ More Fun
- ☐ Nexus
- ☐ Piton Perch
- ☐ Prologue
- ☐ Step Ladder
- ☐ Stinkzig
- ☐ Tarsalation
- ☐ Thin Man
- ☐ TTR

5.7

- ☐ 5.7 Cracks
- ☐ Ascending Colon
- ☐ Big House
- ☐ Candlestick
- ☐ Cold Finger
- ☐ Descending Colon
- ☐ Edwards' Crack
- ☐ Epilog
- ☐ Falcon's Lair
- ☐ Far Right Start
- ☐ Fat Man's Demise
- ☐ Hamburger Crack
- ☐ Handjacker
- ☐ Hassler's Hatbox Route
- ☐ Hole
- ☐ Hypotension
- ☐ Jacquot's Face
- ☐ Jim Jam Junior
- ☐ Journey To Coramonde
- ☐ Kitchen's Delight
- ☐ Klarren
- ☐ Ladder
- ☐ Lichen or Not
- ☐ Lower Slot Left
- ☐ Mother #1
- ☐ MRC Left
- ☐ Nail
- ☐ No Name Chimney
- ☐ Northeast Cutoff
- ☐ Old Eyeful
- ☐ Original Upper Slot Left
- ☐ Outer Notch
- ☐ Recombination Mutation
- ☐ Reverse ? Mark
- ☐ Right Femur
- ☐ Right Start
- ☐ Screw
- ☐ Slat
- ☐ Slit
- ☐ Slut
- ☐ Sugar Crack
- ☐ Ted's Trot
- ☐ TM Chimney
- ☐ Train Leaves at 7
- ☐ Under Achiever
- ☐ Upper Slot
- ☐ W.C.Fields
- ☐ Water Streak
- ☐ Wright of Thick and Thin

5.8

- ☐ Ain't Crack
- ☐ Bad Saturday
- ☐ Baobab Tree
- ☐ Beta Blocker
- ☐ Bombay
- ☐ Button Variation
- ☐ Captain Nemo (Pitch 1)
- ☐ Cat's Cradle
- ☐ Cosmic Debris
- ☐ Damit
- ☐ Dire Pitch
- ☐ Dirty Pictures From Prom
- ☐ Easy Overhang Traverse
- ☐ Existential Dilemma
- ☐ First Gear
- ☐ Flake
- ☐ Friction Slide
- ☐ Gehe Jetzt
- ☐ Get Up That Tree
- ☐ Giggle
- ☐ Golden Grief
- ☐ Hammer
- ☐ Hemoglobin
- ☐ Hesitation
- ☐ Hollerith Exit
- ☐ Humper
- ☐ Kiai
- ☐ Knothole
- ☐ Lawyer On The Toilet
- ☐ Lower Slot
- ☐ Matron
- ☐ Narrow and Ugly
- ☐ Oslund's Delight
- ☐ Par Four
- ☐ Rag--Tag
- ☐ Satterfield's Crack
- ☐ Snap
- ☐ Social Security Ran Out
- ☐ Sore-O-Pod
- ☐ Stem Christy
- ☐ Straight and Narrow
- ☐ Strawberry Jam
- ☐ Tea Grinder
- ☐ Tombstone Crack
- ☐ Top Flight
- ☐ TTL
- ☐ Upper Fall Wall Route
- ☐ Vulture
- ☐ Whirligig Exit
- ☐ Wrist Ranger
- ☐ Zipper

5.9

- [ ] 19th Nervous Breakdown
- [ ] 5.11 Crack
- [ ] Ah! Fair of the Heart
- [ ] Ain't Crack Headwall
- [ ] Arrêtez Maintenant
- [ ] Baalbek
- [ ] Bittersweet
- [ ] Blair Blaster
- [ ] Bolder Exit
- [ ] Bolder Hopper
- [ ] Bombs Away
- [ ] Boulder Hop
- [ ] Cat's Claw
- [ ] CC Left
- [ ] Change of Hand
- [ ] Clean and Jerk
- [ ] Clean and Press
- [ ] Climb and Punishment
- [ ] Coffee Grinder
- [ ] Colorado Cable Cutter
- [ ] Coming Up Short
- [ ] Deception
- [ ] Devil's Food
- [ ] Drip Drop
- [ ] Dual
- [ ] Fallout
- [ ] Fantasia
- [ ] Fear and Loathing
- [ ] Finally
- [ ] Finger Grinder
- [ ] Five Sleazy Creases
- [ ] Flying Right
- [ ] Grunt Layback
- [ ] Guide Book Dilemma
- [ ] Hair Lip
- [ ] Hassler's Right
- [ ] Heads of the Valley
- [ ] Homecoming
- [ ] Horror Show
- [ ] Hurley-Fowler
- [ ] Inside Straight
- [ ] Internal Combustion
- [ ] Intimidation
- [ ] Jet Stream
- [ ] Jim Jam
- [ ] K Exit
- [ ] K.P.
- [ ] Labyrinth
- [ ] Lichentous Wall
- [ ] Lower Progressive
- [ ] Mantle Route
- [ ] Middle Parallel Space
- [ ] Middle Exit
- [ ] Mountaineers Rock Climb
- [ ] MRC Direct
- [ ] Original Horror Show
- [ ] Overload
- [ ] Parade Rest
- [ ] Paul Piana Has A Need...
- [ ] Petit Crapon
- [ ] Plumb Line
- [ ] Pooh Corner (Pitch 1)
- [ ] Popcorn Farce
- [ ] Quits
- [ ] Serpentine
- [ ] Silver Surfer
- [ ] Slant
- [ ] Slot-A-Saurus
- [ ] Straight Edge
- [ ] Strained Tendons
- [ ] Tanfasia
- [ ] Third Time Around
- [ ] Tool or Die
- [ ] Two of a Kind
- [ ] Vacillation Exit
- [ ] Water Streak II

5.10a

- ☐ Altar
- ☐ Arete Aready
- ☐ Blaster Junior
- ☐ Bragging About Jesus
- ☐ Cannonball
- ☐ Cut Off My Legs...
- ☐ Deep Throat
- ☐ Digiripper Raptoris
- ☐ Ejector-Rejector
- ☐ Elevator
- ☐ Failure to Communicate
- ☐ Fall Wall Route
- ☐ Finger Trip Roof
- ☐ First Iteration
- ☐ Flip-Flop and Die
- ☐ Flytrap
- ☐ Folded--Spindled and Mutilated
- ☐ Friday the 13th (Pitch 1)
- ☐ Give Me a Second; I'll...
- ☐ Grand Traverse (Pitch 1)
- ☐ Klink
- ☐ Kopischka Finish
- ☐ Little On The Ugly Side
- ☐ Mainstreet
- ☐ Middle Road
- ☐ Monkey Wrench
- ☐ Moon Tide
- ☐ My Clone Sleeps Alone
- ☐ Neon Madman
- ☐ Outrider
- ☐ Pod Awful
- ☐ Ralph Called
- ☐ Rubber Biscuit
- ☐ S.S. Maywood
- ☐ Skull
- ☐ Slash
- ☐ Spastic Colitis
- ☐ Stand and Deliver
- ☐ Storm Watch
- ☐ Tat Exit
- ☐ Through Thick and Thin
- ☐ Upper Progressive
- ☐ Vault
- ☐ Vulture Direct
- ☐ Who The Devil is ...
- ☐ Zigzag

5.10b

- ☐ In The Groove
- ☐ Inside Flush
- ☐ Bad Girls Do
- ☐ Bat Drop Crack
- ☐ Beef Eater
- ☐ Best of the Blues
- ☐ Buttox
- ☐ Citadel Crack
- ☐ Currey's Diagonal
- ☐ Escalator
- ☐ Flaming Blue Jesus
- ☐ Flying Buttress
- ☐ Gash
- ☐ Gloria's Fantasy
- ☐ Hard To Believe
- ☐ Hello Stupid
- ☐ Knee Grinder
- ☐ Orbital Ridge
- ☐ Pooh Corner
- ☐ Putter
- ☐ Raised On Robbery
- ☐ Sorority Girl
- ☐ Stress Fracture
- ☐ Thing of Beauty
- ☐ Upper Slot Left
- ☐ Victory of Defeat
- ☐ Wild Thing

5.10c

- ☐ 12th of Never
- ☐ Bat Heaven
- ☐ Church Not Made By Hands
- ☐ Connecticut Yankee
- ☐ Das Boot
- ☐ Dreaming of Babylon
- ☐ Flake-O-Saurus
- ☐ Grand Traverse
- ☐ Grief Roof
- ☐ H
- ☐ Hooker
- ☐ Jay's Solo
- ☐ Master Blaster
- ☐ Micky Mantle
- ☐ Penis Dimension
- ☐ Poker Face
- ☐ Seam Variation
- ☐ Tri-cera-tops I
- ☐ Tri-cera-tops II
- ☐ Tri-cera-tops III

5.10d

- ☐ Atherolichenous Plaque
- ☐ Captain Nemo
- ☐ Cool Hand Luke
- ☐ Date With a Dike
- ☐ Japan Club
- ☐ Left Torpedo Tube
- ☐ Lichen Lung
- ☐ Medium Cool
- ☐ Moonrise Variation
- ☐ Rocking Chair
- ☐ Ultra Violets

5.11a

- [ ] Argon Depressive
- [ ] Aspen Stem
- [ ] B-G Crack
- [ ] Balls Out
- [ ] Bell Crack
- [ ] Black and Decker
- [ ] Colonial Rule
- [ ] Cross Bones
- [ ] Cyber-Way
- [ ] Emperor of Wyoming
- [ ] Father #1
- [ ] Fever Dreams
- [ ] Flake Out
- [ ] Flare Thee Well
- [ ] Friday the 13th (Pitch 2)
- [ ] Friday the 13th--Part II
- [ ] Gunga Din
- [ ] Horn's Mother
- [ ] Howling
- [ ] Hung Like A Horse
- [ ] It's OK To Be Humbled
- [ ] Krypton Sociopath
- [ ] Last of the Elfin Boltmen
- [ ] Little Stone
- [ ] Mandela
- [ ] MaxiLash
- [ ] Misfits
- [ ] Nitrogen Narcosis
- [ ] Orange Christmas
- [ ] Piece of Dirt
- [ ] Pollyanna Goes To Hell
- [ ] Rainbow in the Dark
- [ ] Route of All Evil
- [ ] Sky Shot
- [ ] Spandex
- [ ] Wide and Ugly

5.11b

- [ ] Automotive Supply House
- [ ] Bad Girl's Dream
- [ ] Behind Blue Eyes
- [ ] Big Pink
- [ ] Blade Runner
- [ ] Boardwalk
- [ ] Burning Spear
- [ ] Calling On You--Moscow
- [ ] Castles in the Sand
- [ ] Central Scrutinizer
- [ ] Exit Ramp
- [ ] Eye of Fatima
- [ ] Frankenstine
- [ ] Ghost Dance
- [ ] Gloria
- [ ] Good-bye White Opel
- [ ] Granite Stairway
- [ ] Hesitation Blues
- [ ] I
- [ ] I'm Spartacus
- [ ] Light From Blue Horses
- [ ] Little Creatures
- [ ] Mud In Your Eye
- [ ] Never Ending Story
- [ ] October Light
- [ ] Passover
- [ ] Rising Sun
- [ ] Ruffis
- [ ] Solo For Swallows
- [ ] Spider God
- [ ] Strong Love
- [ ] Very Bad Saturday
- [ ] War Zone
- [ ] What the French Girl Said
- [ ] When You're Strange
- [ ] Worm Drive
- [ ] Zealot

5.11c

- [ ] Blood Sport
- [ ] Call Me Barney
- [ ] Climbs of Passion Exit
- [ ] Cool Jet
- [ ] Crichton's Crack
- [ ] Deadman's Glove
- [ ] Drees Special
- [ ] Garden of Earthly Delights
- [ ] Gravity's Rainbow
- [ ] Hume-Annoyed From Dixie
- [ ] Max Factor
- [ ] Moonsault
- [ ] Muscle and Fitness
- [ ] Old Dog's New Trick
- [ ] Pretzel Logic
- [ ] Proctologist
- [ ] Right Torpedo Tube
- [ ] Scarlet Begonias
- [ ] Soft Parade
- [ ] SpectreMan
- [ ] Superb Arete
- [ ] Tips and Asps
- [ ] Whaling on Napalm

5.11d

- [ ] Arch Stanton
- [ ] Bug Squad
- [ ] Crankenstine
- [ ] Eleven Cent Moon
- [ ] Flying Ants
- [ ] Friday Blues
- [ ] Friday the 13th
- [ ] Jihad
- [ ] London Calling
- [ ] Mystery Blocks(?)
- [ ] SB
- [ ] Static Cling
- [ ] Still A Gorilla

5.12a

- [ ] Drunken Redneck Rappelers
- [ ] Easter Island
- [ ] Finger Fantasy
- [ ] Fourth of July Crack
- [ ] I'd Rather Be in Philadelphia
- [ ] June Bride,
- [ ] Nasty Crack
- [ ] Pipeline
- [ ] Reading Raymond Chandler
- [ ] Rookie
- [ ] Space Oddity
- [ ] Tragically Hip
- [ ] Veda-Voodoo

5.12b

☐ Air Voyager With Report
☐ Every Move You Make
☐ Harder Than Your Husband
☐ Hypertension
☐ Master of Sport
☐ Mr. Chimp

☐ New Maps of Hell
☐ Pretty Girls With Long Knives
☐ Remote Control
☐ Squat
☐ Trip Master Monkey
☐ Whistling Jupiter

5.12c/d

☐ Caesar
☐ Cross of Iron

☐ New Mutant
☐ Slick and Superficial

5.13a/b

☐ Lucille
☐ North Shore
☐ Panther of the Weak

☐ Silver Salute
☐ Young Guns

Index

The general index lists all the routes and most other items for which a page number might be handy. If a route has more than one name in general use, both names will be found in the index with a cross reference to the preferred name. General items are listed as in the following example. Page number references are in *italics.*

Walt's Wall Area, *13, 21.*

This means there are references to "Walt's Wall Area" on pages 13 and 21.

Routes are listed as in the following example.

When You're Strange 11b, *155.*

This means that "When You're Strange" is rated 5.11b and that there is a reference to it on page 155.

If an item, referenced on more than one page, has one of the pages listed in **boldface**, it means that page is the dominant reference. In the case of a route, it would be the page on which the route description occurs. This is illustrated in the following examples.

Coke Bottle, *13, 21, **27**, 33.*

This means "Coke Bottle" is referenced on pages, 13, 21, 27, and 33 with the reference on page 27 being the most important.

Drunken Redneck ... 12a, *14, 85, **90***

This means that "Drunken Redneck ... " is rated 12a, has references on pages 14, 85, and 90. The reference on page 90 is the route description. Note the use of the ellipsis "..." to shorten the name. This is done for route names that are longer than 20 characters.

H

I

J

inner STRENGTH rock gym

Come Enjoy the Comforts
and Challenges of
Indoor Climbing!

Inner Strength Rock Gym

3713 S. Mason St.
Ft. Collins, CO 80525
(303)282-8118

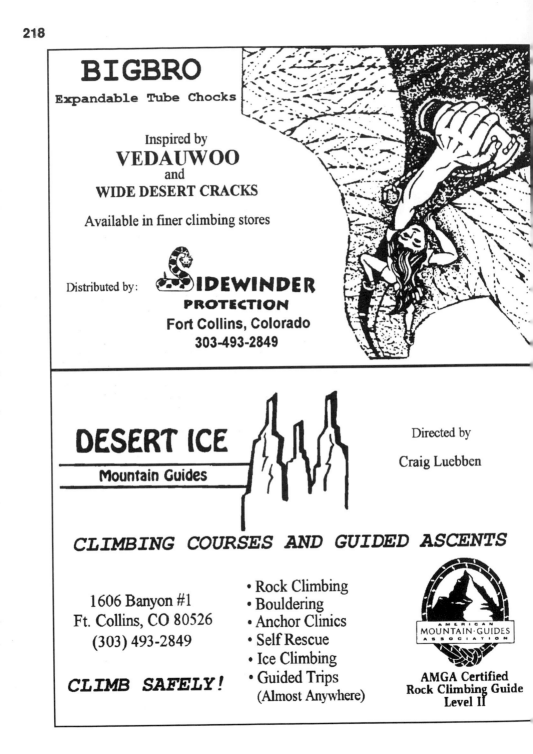

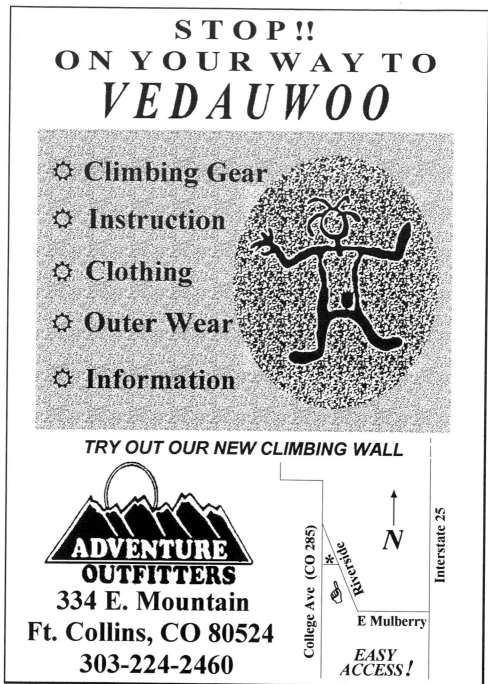

NOTES

"Climbing is not a sport, it is a way of life.
The way you get to the top expresses
who you are,
your values and the type of life
you are living.
Climbing takes place in nature,
it is a school of life."

(P. Edlinger)

NOTES

NOTES

"Climbing can be important for anyone. It can teach you how to concentrate, how to reach a goal, and it can change your perspective of yourself. **People are too used to living in the horizontal plane."** (C. Destivelle)

NOTES

NOTES

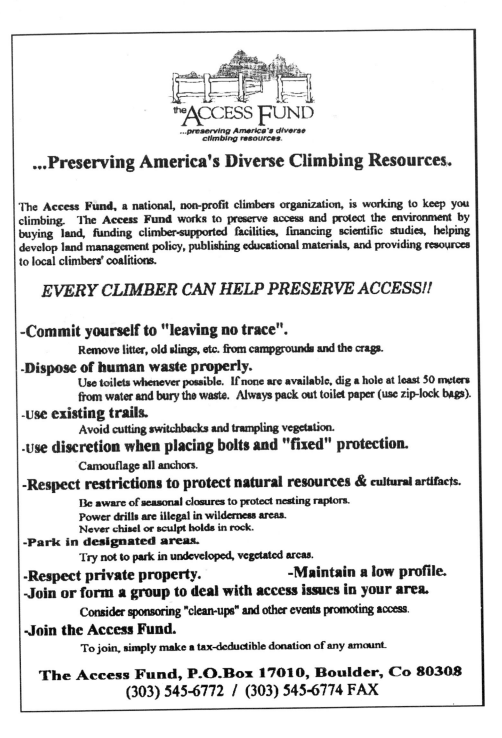

...Preserving America's Diverse Climbing Resources.

The **Access Fund**, a national, non-profit climbers organization, is working to keep you climbing. The **Access Fund** works to preserve access and protect the environment by buying land, funding climber-supported facilities, financing scientific studies, helping develop land management policy, publishing educational materials, and providing resources to local climbers' coalitions.

EVERY CLIMBER CAN HELP PRESERVE ACCESS!!

-Commit yourself to "leaving no trace".
> Remove litter, old slings, etc. from campgrounds and the crags.

-Dispose of human waste properly.
> Use toilets whenever possible. If none are available, dig a hole at least 50 meters from water and bury the waste. Always pack out toilet paper (use zip-lock bags).

-Use existing trails.
> Avoid cutting switchbacks and trampling vegetation.

-Use discretion when placing bolts and "fixed" protection.
> Camouflage all anchors.

-Respect restrictions to protect natural resources & cultural artifacts.
> Be aware of seasonal closures to protect nesting raptors.
> Power drills are illegal in wilderness areas.
> Never chisel or sculpt holds in rock.

-Park in designated areas.
> Try not to park in undeveloped, vegetated areas.

-Respect private property.   **-Maintain a low profile.**

-Join or form a group to deal with access issues in your area.
> Consider sponsoring "clean-ups" and other events promoting access.

-Join the Access Fund.
> To join, simply make a tax-deductible donation of any amount.

The Access Fund, P.O.Box 17010, Boulder, Co 80308
(303) 545-6772 / (303) 545-6774 FAX